THE
SELLER'S
CHALLENGE

PRAISE FOR *THE SELLER'S CHALLENGE*

"As a sales leader in the medical device sector, I am commonly approached by candidates wanting to know how to get into this fast-paced, relationship driven, financially rewarding, and patient outcomes-focused industry.

I have now found the perfect book for each of them to read and use as a reference throughout the lifecycle of their sales career. Even as a tenured seller, I found this book to be a fantastic resource. While it contains some great fundamental reminders, this is the first sales book I've seen take the 'art of sales' to a new level thanks to detailed, real-life stories, chapter takeaways, and checklists/worksheets to be used when the situation arises. The best part about this book is you can read a chapter before a big RFP or Value Analysis Committee and be ready for battle without having to reread the entire book. The authors (Tom Williams and Tom Saine) did their homework on this one!"

Al Kepler,
Vice President ENT, Smith & Nephew

"Gaining a seat at the executive table has become tougher and tougher, *The Seller's Challenge* provides a brilliant roadmap to help sales professionals rise above the status quo. In complex business environments with multiple decision makers and influencers, sales professionals will learn new strategies to enhance their skillset fueling their long-term success. A definite read and continual reference guide for sales professionals."

Larry Levine,
Author of *Selling From The Heart—How Your Authentic Self Sells You*,
Co-host of the Selling From The Heart podcast

"I have just finished reading *The Seller's Challenge* by authors Thomas Williams and Thomas Saine. When I read sales books, I am always looking for the parts of the book that alter or enhance my thinking. *The Seller's Challenge* really got into my sales brain with its deconstruction of 1) Gate Keepers and 2) Procurement. Brilliant work here and jam packed with great stories, graphs, detail, and recommendations! "The Seller's Challenge profoundly appealed to my analytical self. I love sales books that pull long held arguments on sales topics apart and then reconstructs them with navigation and management tips. Buy this book and pull out a box of highlighters…. you are going to need them!"

Patrick Tinney,
Author of *Perpetual Hunger and Unlocking Yes*

"If you deal with a B2B complex sale, this book is a must read. It's current and teaches you how to align your sales process with the ways customers/clients are buying today. The authors do a great job giving you a road map to build a strategy for sales success."

William L. MacDonald,
CEO of Plein Aire Strategies, Best-Selling Author of *MERGE* and new release of *MERGE 2.0*

"*The Seller's Challenge* provides many unique perspectives to mastering 10 deal killing obstacles found in today's complex selling environment. Cleverly designed and extremely thorough, this book provides unique insights and real-life solutions to the toughest issues encountered by today's B2B salespeople. Salespeople love shortcuts and those same salespeople will be able to select a single chapter of the book that addresses the problem they're facing and find solutions they can use to help them shorten their sales cycle and close those key deals!"

Stephen J. Bistritz Ed.D.,
Co-author of *Selling to the C-Suite*

"*The Seller's Challenge* is an excellent guide that first explains the top ten challenges that professional sellers face today and then shows how it's best to deal with them. The book is filled with tips, ideas and recommended action to perform. Tom & Tom shared their expertise, knowledge, and insights in every page of this book. Must read!"

Lahat Tzvi,
CEO of Tfisot—Sales Consulting Group

"There are two paths to learning how to overcome obstacles in complex B2B sales: Spend 30 years overcoming those obstacles yourself as Tom Williams and Tom Saine have done or learn from their stories and fabulous insights. I recommend you read *The Seller's Challenge* and save yourself the decades of effort"

Mike Adams,
Author *Seven Stories Every Salesperson Must Tell*

"If you are new to B2B sales or are simply finding the current environment more difficult than ever in which to compete, *The Seller's Challenge* is a great resource for you right now. This is a practical reference guide written by two experienced and very successful practitioners who have found repeatable ways to overcome the most difficult challenges sellers face. This is the kind of book you don't just read once. You can pick it up any time you need guidance on how to overcome a difficult situation, and you can take Williams and Saine's advice to the bank."

Matthew McDarby,
Author of *The Cadence of Excellence: Key Habits of Effective Sales Managers*

"Every year there are significant changes in the market that sales people must adapt to for success. In *The Seller's Challenge*, Thomas Williams and Thomas Saine provide a series of thoughtful strategic and tactical best practices that force even the most experienced sales person to challenge their own thinking and common assumptions. If you're selling in a complex market, you must make time to read this book!"

Steve Gielda,
Author of *Premeditated Selling* and Co-Founder of Ignite Selling

"Want the raw, unvarnished truth about selling today? If you've been indoctrinated with traditional sales methods, you might not like it. Yet, if you're willing to discontinue the old-school tactics that stopped working a decade ago, and start doing what really works today, study this masterful book. Tom Williams and Tom Saine take on the toughest sales problems, frequently caused by bad sales training and poor sales habits, and show you exactly how to break through to master modern selling methods. What's the biggest challenge you face? It's probably thinking that the old game still works. Learn the new game and start winning deals again. "

Mark S.A. Smith,
Author of *MSP to BSP: Pivot to Profit from IT Disruption*,
Host of the Selling Disruption Show podcast

"Written for the B2B seller who operates in a high-stakes sales environment, *The Sellers Challenge* provides a series of practical, tactical treatments of how to prepare for, manage, negotiate, and close deals in the face of ten common sales situations. It focuses on understandings and actions that are within the seller's personal control and, I believe, will prove especially useful to those who deal with large, bureaucratic accounts in single locations. The book clearly derives from deep personal experience with sellers and benefits from interesting case stories and detailed recommendations."

Barbara Weaver Smith,
Co-Author of *The Whale Hunters*,
Author of *"Whale Hunting With Global Accounts*
and Founder & CEO, The Whale Hunters, Inc.

"*The Seller's Challenge* is an outstanding book and I highly recommend it! Tom Williams and Tom Saine have succinctly captured the challenges sales professionals face in today's environment. They have created a "crew resource management guide"– 10 chapters that will help sales professionals focus on interpersonal communication, planning, leadership, and decision making that occurs on both sides of the aisle during the sales process."

Glen Hall,
Vice President Business Development, Sg2

Williams and Saine have been able to break down the barriers and techniques to overcome challenges experienced by all sales professionals. *The Seller's Challenge* tests assumptions, builds differentiation and demonstrates the importance of thoughtful planning to deliver true customer value.

Their stories are relevant and takes the reader through ten disciplines that will increase win ratios, time to close and overall sales performance. An excellent read for a new sales representative or seasoned veteran.

Jamie Gallagher
Vice President Distributor Relations & Channel Management, BD—Canada

THE SELLER'S CHALLENGE

HOW TOP SELLERS MASTER 10 DEAL KILLING OBSTACLES IN B2B SALES

By Thomas Williams and Thomas Saine

The Seller's Challenge: How Top Sellers Master 10 Deal Killing Obstacles in B2B Sales
Copyright © 2018 by Thomas J. Williams, Tom Saine and Strategic Dynamics Inc. All Rights Reserved.

For information about this title or to order other books and/or electronic media, contact the publisher:
Complex Sale Publishing
Thomas Williams
Thomas Saine
Strategic Dynamics Inc.
twilliams@strategicdynamicsfirm.com

978-1-948974-00-4 (hardcover)
978-1-948974-02-8 (softcover)
978-1-948974-01-1 (eBook)

Printed in the United States of America

Table of Contents

Dedication

This book is dedicated to Bob Miller, co-founder of Miller Heiman Inc. Visionary, Author, Mentor, and Friend

Foreword

In over thirty years of sales I have had the privilege to serve in every sales capacity—from individual contributor to Executive VP of Sales. And in that time, I have had the opportunity to learn all the major sales systems in the marketplace. I have found merit in every sales methodology I have encountered. Yet, in training my own teams and training for others, I have found that regardless of the approach and sales methodology there is a consistent set of challenges that continue to crop up. And as reliable as the rising sun, one or more of these challenges will make its appearance in the middle of whatever workshop you are conducting. They are important and often immediate needs for sales professionals. Yet the irony is that they fall outside the scope of virtually all the major sales systems. They live in a strange sort of no-man's land—too specific to be addressed by a general methodology and too complex and time-consuming to be covered in a public offering. And as a result, they rarely get addressed.

This is the reason I was so excited to see that Thomas Williams and Thomas Saine had collected and written a best-practices guide for the top ten of these important-but-rarely-addressed challenges for sales professionals. That guide is *The Seller's Challenge: How Top Sellers Master 10 Deal Killing Obstacles in B2B Sales.*

I know Tom and Tom from the world of business to business selling. Tom Williams and I both hail from the healthcare world where Tom has the rare quality of having sat on both sides of the table as a successful sales professional as well as the CEO of two specialty hospitals. Tom Saine hails from ARAMARK where he served in many executive positions including Vice President of Sales and brings a truly unique contribution in sales communication. Together they are uniquely qualified to write about these challenges and the best way to navigate them from both the professional buyer and seller's perspective.

The Seller's Challenge is relevant to every business to business sales professional. Not only does it cover the 10 biggest challenges in B2B sales, but it does so thoroughly. Within these pages are the answer to the following questions:

- What is the best way to sell to the multiple buyers that are within every complex sale?
- What is the best way to research, plan and execute a sales call that moves the buying process forward?
- How do I influence buyers who are already strongly committed to a different course of action?
- Why are my sales calls bombing out? What is the root cause and how can I fix it?
- What is the best way to address gatekeepers and how can I leverage them to gain access to executive buyers?
- Why is the status quo my #1 competitor and how do I create an effective strategy to compete against it?
- When should I participate in a Request for Proposal and how can I build a strategy that overcomes the limitations of the dysfunctional RFP process?
- Why is selling to committees so hard and what is the best way to develop and execute a committee-focused sales strategy?
- How do I manage and collaborate with procurement in a way that creates success?
- What is the best way to manage price and discount demands?

One or more of these questions is guaranteed to come up in every workshop. And the best thing? The answers in *The Seller's Challenge* are phenomenal. You can tell that Williams and Saine have run sales workshops for years because each chapter contains all the resources needed to train the topic in its own self-contained workshop. Each section contains:

- A summary of the challenge
- A story illustrating the challenge
- A discussion of the challenge along with a breakdown of the dynamics involved
- An illustration or model
- The solution and best practice in addressing the challenge and recommended actions
- A Summary of Key Points to Remember
- And commitment & action items to incorporate the best practice into your selling process

There are also generally one or two addendums at the end of each chapter illustrating exactly how to implement the best practice in a real-world story. These often contain valuable reference materials such as additional resources and checklists. And finally, there is a downloadable companion workbook that follows each chapter and subject at: https://strategicdynamicsfirm.com/the-sellers-chal…mpanion-workbook/

As a VP of Sales and an experienced workshop facilitator I can tell you that *The Seller's Challenge* is a dream come true. It is the most complete treatment of these topics I have found anywhere, and the "best news" is each of the chapters will be available as an individual or combined workshop and eventually via eLearning through Strategic Dynamics.

For that reason, I was excited to write the foreword to *The Seller's Challenge*. If you have ever read great works like Strategic Selling, SPIN Selling or The Challenger Sale you will appreciate (like I did) how *The Seller's Challenge* complements these classic systems. It's everything I look for in a book—it's practical, actionable, explains the "why" behind the recommended practices and delivers everything necessary to put the best-practices into action. If you are in business to business sales, then you've likely encountered every one of these challenges and herein lays the best approach for navigating each one. Embracing these practices will generate more sales and more revenue by eliminating the obstacles and pitfalls that kill so many B2B sales.

James Muir—CEO of Best Practice International

and Best-Selling Author of *The Perfect Close*

Introduction

SELL OUTSIDE YOUR COMFORT ZONE

Just like other segments of the population, sales professionals have trouble getting rid of bad habits. In fact, some behaviors were probably good habits in their day. It's just that times have changed and our behaviors have remained the same. We have gotten comfortable doing something one way and see no reason for change. Well . . . get over it. That's what professionals do. No matter how uncomfortable or uneasy we may feel, change is essential to personal growth. It's time to break out of your comfort zone, take a fresh view of your customer's needs, and adapt to the new world of challenges that are facing you.

Sales is the most vital point of interface between selling and buying organizations. As sellers, we have to be the quickest to adapt and implement change. We are closely connected to our customers—more so than any other function of our organization. When our customers are plagued by aggressive competition, failed product releases, and eroding profit margin, we are the problem solvers, change managers, and therapists who arrive unsolicited and (often) unwanted. We help our customers discover threats, grasp opportunities, find new resources, and implement solutions. We are the unseen turnaround specialists who navigate mine fields or hazards, including the built-in resistance of the buying organization.

We are faced with changing not only our customer's behavior but changing our own. Saying we need to change is simple. Changing our behavior can be challenging.

Recently a colleague introduced us to Destin Sandlin's *Backward Brain Bicycle* (check out YouTube Backward Brain Bicycle on Smarter Every Day). Destin tells of his journey in attempting to learn how to ride a bicycle. Only this bicycle had one difference from the normal bicycles that we learned to ride as children. The bicycle was engineered so that when he turned the handlebars in one direction, the bicycle's front tire turned in the opposite direction. The question was: how long would it take to learn how to ride the backward bicycle? You may find the answer hard to believe. It took 8 weeks of daily practice. It connected, slowly at first. Then faster. Finally, he mastered the backward bicycle. Destin explains an important aspect of learning. He says, "Once you have a rigid way of thinking in your head sometimes you can't change it even if you want to." Throughout our lives, we repeat and reinforce habits daily—both good and bad.

We build a neurological algorithm of actions and movements that we reinforce throughout our lives. There is an old axiom that applies: "Just because you know what to do doesn't mean you know how to do it." If change and adaptation are constant forces in the lives of sales professionals, it's foolish to think that we can change quickly or easily. If you want to plow the neurological pathways for better conversation with buyers, then be willing to plan and practice. It will come with effort.

(Oh, by the way, it took Destin's seven-year-old son two weeks to learn how to ride the backward bicycle).

So what exactly is the purpose of *The Seller's Challenge*? It's to share advice and explore options, to overcome myths and wrongful perceptions, and to plot a different course of action—one that may require new skills and will certainly require different approaches to understanding and engaging your customers. This book is intended to help you overcome the 10 most frequent obstacles in complex B2B selling. Because each chapter stands on its own, this book can be read in different ways. Some sellers may elect to read each chapter in the order presented. Other sellers may elect to read only the chapters that directly apply to their sales environment. Finally, some sellers may select the key chapters they believe could provide some immediate answers to thorny issues they are dealing with today.

JOIN THE COMMUNITY OF SCHOLARS

This book was never intended to compete with or replace those great books on sales methodology. In this regard, we are "agnostic." The inspiration for this book came from the questions raised by sales professionals like yourself in workshops over the past fifteen years—questions that surfaced at lunch, over coffee, at breaks, during dinner, and from quite a few desperate evening phone calls. Most of these questions are tactical in nature, focused on a specific obstacle or two. This book does not pretend to provide the best thinking on these issues—just *our* best thinking from working with sales professionals from many industries around the world. Our goal is to enable you to improve vital sales skills and master the restraints that limit your effectiveness and obstruct your success.

If you want to grow as a sales professional, become a participant in the growing community of scholars. Read books, articles, and blogs. Listen to webinars, podcasts, and audio books. Participate in online conversations. If you hold an impassioned position on an issue, then write, publish, or respond. Become a voice for yourself and your teammates. You'll find that it's a wonderful two-way street. You will become both teacher and student—just as others will learn from you, you will learn from them.

BECOME CUSTOMER READY

If there is a common thread among the thousands of hours of conversation we've held with sales representatives and managers, it's that far too many sales professionals lack vital knowledge of their customers. Yet customers are desperate to find professionals who can share insights on issues that trouble them daily. As one executive put it, "We seldom meet an account manager or channel partner who wants to talk about our needs—just their products."

We are quick to declare ourselves "customer ready" when we haven't researched our customer's challenges or developed a strategy around our customer's buying process. Our premise is that the key to selling effectively lies in discovering who is buying, how they want to buy, and what the solution will do for their organization. This means mapping sales activity to the customer's buying process. That is the only way to become truly customer ready. This takes hard work and perseverance. Consider that, for certain buying decisions, a given customer may find themselves in a position of deciding on a product once every seven years (example: equipment). The sales representative and their company may help other customers navigate the same decision process seven or more times every year. Very often the customer is going through a learning journey as they discover what they need to consider in the buying process. This creates a unique opportunity for the sales representative to provide insight or perspective and position himself as a "trusted advisor."

Professional development is a lifelong struggle. We want so much to believe in our own competence that we turn a blind eye to our shortcomings. Over coffee, sales professionals complain about their golf handicap, report on articles from *Golf Digest* and tell of their plans to purchase new clubs. They invest hours on driving ranges and putting greens. What if we applied the same interest and discipline to our profession? What if we read more, identified our deficiencies, and practiced important skills?

We have a close friend who is a golf fanatic. Several years ago, he created a tournament, with a new twist. When participants registered for the tournament they were given a four-foot length of string along with one pair of scissors for every foursome. The string allowed the player to "comp" a putt if the distance from the ball to the hole was no greater than the length of string. Here's the catch: every time you "comped" a putt, you had to cut off the amount of string that's equal to the distance from the ball to the hole. As the round of golf progressed, players found their length of string getting shorter and shorter. The challenge was to decide where to invest your string. That's your challenge as well.

Most sports are games of "inches." Sales is a profession of degrees. If you want more string—you've got to earn it. Become connected with your customers, understand how they wish to buy, discover underlying needs, and build road maps that make purchasing easy. Every step you take that allows you to become more connected to your customer adds inches to your string. If you undertake a thorough study of your customer, it will prove its value in every question you ask, in every statement you make, and in every insight you offer. Your challenge isn't to become customer-facing. Quite frankly, everyone has gone down that road. Your challenge is to become "customer intimate." As Robert Frost wrote, that's "the road not taken."

Good luck and good selling.

Tom Williams

Tom Saine

Chapter 1

Selling to Multiple Buyers

"Who Buys?" "Who Cares?" "What Matters?"

"Your strategy can only begin when you know who the key players are."
Bob Miller—Co-author of *The New Strategic Selling*

Three seemingly simple questions lie at the heart of why sellers win or lose. "Who buys?" "Who cares?" "What matters?" If you don't know or aren't sure of the answers, you may be in for a bumpy ride. "Who buys?" addresses the question of which executive or committee has the formal responsibility to authorize the purchase. Sellers who discover the function or role each stakeholder will play in the buying process will benefit from that knowledge. "Who cares?" points the seller toward influencers and those receptive to change. "What matters?" prompts the question of why a buyer or buying group would select you. Buyers consider the value you offer and how you have differentiated yourself from the competition. If you know what matters most to buyers, you can leverage that knowledge to build support.

In some sales opportunities, these questions are easily answered. In other situations, the task of sorting through stakeholders and buyers can be confusing and time consuming. The questions, "Who buys?" "Who cares?" "What matters?" belie an enormous challenge for sellers in many industries. For example, consider the challenges posed by a new and unexpected member of a buying committee in the story below.

Story: Consulting Services

Several years ago, Jim was approached by an existing client and asked to provide additional project services. He identified all the key players and performed his due diligence. Since this was a long-term client and the client approached him, he assumed this was a "slam dunk" sales opportunity. Nevertheless, Jim did his homework. Before he presented his findings and recommendations, he asked for a meeting with everyone.

The client provided a date and a distribution list that included a name Jim didn't recognize. Jim inquired and learned the name belonged to a new consultant who had been onboard for only a week. He was told not to worry and that, "She's been brought up to speed on our relationship with your company." Jim checked her LinkedIn profile and saw it included a recommendation from one of his competitors.

When Jim tried to meet with her before the presentation, she didn't have time. Can you guess what happened? She tried to undermine Jim's position in favor of the competitor. Although she was not successful, it caused a bit of consternation, and Jim's preparation enabled him to anticipate and maneuver around this obstacle.

The lesson: Identify all stakeholders, their alliances, and their vested interests.

Seller's Challenge: *Identify All Stakeholders and Build an In-Depth Profile That Will Help Prioritize and Customize Sales Activity*

When more stakeholders and buyers complicate the buying process, sellers are challenged to identify all the stakeholders involved—including their functions or roles in the decision process, their vested interests, and their intent to advocate one product over another.

Most opportunities have been lost because a stakeholder, unknown to the seller, provided input that undermined the seller's competitive position. In this chapter, we explore the challenges of identifying key stakeholders, and we introduce a mapping process to help sellers identify buyers, their mindset and urgency to change, influence, accessibility, who desires the seller's solution versus the competition's, and the decision criteria.

To better understand stakeholder mapping, we'll explore the difficulties sellers encounter when identifying stakeholders and the challenges sellers face when they sell to multiple buyers or stakeholders. We'll examine six questions that sellers must answer about each stakeholder. In Addendum 1 we'll show (in story format) the benefits and utility of a Stakeholder Mapping Worksheet.

WHY IS IT DIFFICULT TO IDENTIFY KEY STAKEHOLDERS?

There are two overriding reasons why sellers find it difficult to identify key stakeholders in the buying process: First, sellers never bother to "map" the buying process in the target organization. Without that vital information, it's difficult to appreciate how multi-layered a buying process can become. Sales representatives often assume that the buying process for one product is the same as for other products or prior purchases. That assumption leads sellers in the wrong direction, wasting valuable time with people who have little or no impact on the buying decision. Second, buying processes across industries are becoming more formal and complex—often controlled by committees and teams. This chapter will help sellers identify and attend to the increasing complexity of the buying process.

Corporate Collaboration & Larger Selection Teams

As organizations grow, they are faced with the challenge of managing their own internal complexity. Instead of having one product that solves multiple problems, they are faced with multiple solutions to a single problem. At the C-suite level, they address complex questions: how to overcome increasing technological complexity, minimize process duplication, focus on fiscal responsiveness, and comply with regulatory mandates while avoiding unnecessary risk. The C-suite answers these questions through organizational collaboration. To achieve collaboration and reduce risk, companies populate buying teams with executives, technical specialists, consultants, and channel partners.

A recent study by CEB (now CEB-Gartner) reported that from 2015 to 2017 the average number of stakeholders directly involved in buying processes increased from 5.4 to 6.8.[1] The implication is that it takes longer to schedule, brief, and survey teams as sizes increase. This results in a longer resource-intensive sales cycle. To promote executive-level collaboration, many executives have opened buying-committee participation to representatives from various user groups and technical specialties. It is easier to avoid blame or criticism when you've included every stakeholder imaginable.

Mergers, Acquisitions, & Expansion

Mergers, acquisitions, and global expansion present buying challenges for many corporations. "Should we include our new partners?" "Should we standardize our buying processes across all newly acquired teams?" From the seller's perspective, there is no assurance that last year's buying team or process will be the same as this year's.

Expanding Role of Procurement

In most organizations, Procurement is being pushed to assume a greater role in the oversight and management of buying processes. Faced with financial headwinds and a mandate to preserve cash, Procurement has become the force behind standardization, score carding, cost containment, and RFPs. In some instances, Procurement groups advocate dividing contracts among several suppliers to ensure continuous price competition. In situations where a supplier provides a highly differentiated, dominant product, Procurement is quick to forge contracts that ensure an uninterrupted supply of product.

With more stakeholders than ever contributing to the buying process, it may be easier for sellers to ask, "Who's not on the committee?" From Procurement's perspective, they are concerned that vital supplies and services won't get purchased or delivered on time. It has become a serious challenge for both buyer and seller.

WHAT CHALLENGES DO SELLERS FACE?

Let's consider the broad array of challenges sellers face due to the combination of forces we have described.

- **Sellers are faced with more stakeholders to identify and contact.** Sales cycles are longer and require more resources—the same resources that are in demand for multiple selling opportunities in the same sales funnel. It's difficult for sellers to allocate their time and forecast accurately when the buying process continues to lengthen.
- **The larger the team of buyers, the higher the likelihood the buying process will stall or fail to reach a suitable solution.** When sellers are faced with a single buying agent, the buying process has approximately an 80% chance of culminating in a purchase. When faced with 2 buying agents, the probability of reaching a buying decision drops to around 55%. At 6 buyers, the chance of reaching a satisfactory resolution falls to a little more than 30%.[2]
- **Sellers will need more internal supporters (sponsors) to manage and answer stakeholder concerns.** It used to be the case that sellers were well positioned if they could develop a single sponsor or advocate on a three-person buying team. When the list of stakeholders grows to 5 or 8 and each has different priorities, functions, and geographies, sellers must drive consensus among the stakeholders.

If sellers fail to take responsibility for driving consensus, who will? The result will be a funnel filled with stalled opportunities.

- **Sellers are faced with less-transparent buying processes.** Increased formality often means limited access. Sellers have limited information about the buyers, the function each performs, and the information the buyers need to make decisions.

- **Sellers need to establish good working relationships with Procurement.** As organizations turn to Procurement to standardize and manage buying processes, Procurement executives are challenged by many of the same issues facing the seller: size, complexity, information flow, and common decision criteria. The challenge for sellers is to build strong working relationships with the Procurement team. The focal issue isn't, "How can I get around, past, or through Procurement?" The challenge is, "How can I help Procurement do their job, so they'll help me do mine?"

- **Sellers find it necessary to deploy teams to execute their sales strategy.** This calls for an early assessment of essential resources. If sellers fail to grasp the enormity of the challenge early on, they may find themselves outnumbered, outflanked, out of time, and out of options. The gravity of this situation is multiplied many times for enterprise sellers faced with mergers, acquisitions, and global sales opportunities.

- **Sellers face buying committees that conduct their own research and discovery.** As buying committees and teams become laden with technical specialists, buyers are launching product-performance and integrity tests instead of relying on sellers for data. Companies are hiring Procurement agents who specialize in purchasing high-ticket products such as IT, manufacturing, energy, transportation, etc.

Almost all sellers begin to develop their strategy by focusing on the "Who buys?" question. As we all know, it's a deceptively simple question, one that requires guidance and validation. Even the most successful sellers can share more than one story about being misled or deceived.

Here's what's wrong with the current process that many sellers follow: They begin by assuming that only one or two stakeholders are involved. "Let's not make this more complicated than it needs to be." They keep an open mind (and ear) for new input that suggests the addition of more or different stakeholders. Then someone mentions a new stakeholder, and our seller begins tracking that person. Then another name comes to light. By the time the seller realizes that the buying team is much larger than anticipated and the process is much more complicated, they have lost the advantage of time. Now the seller might find other mistaken assumptions about who has ultimate authority to award the business or who favors which solution.

We need to go well beyond the single question ("Who buys?") and expand the scope of our discovery process while drilling down to determine the function performed by each stakeholder in the buying process.

WHAT IS "STAKEHOLDER MAPPING?"

Stakeholder mapping is a process designed to identify the key stakeholders, users, specialists, and third-party influencers involved in the buying and decision process. By correctly mapping and profiling stakeholders, a seller can ensure that each buyer is identified along with their role in the decision process. Some stakeholders may have a "drop by" or temporary role, while others are charged with managing the process and reporting to senior executives.

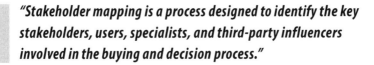

> *"Stakeholder mapping is a process designed to identify the key stakeholders, users, specialists, and third-party influencers involved in the buying and decision process."*

Mapping helps the seller create a comprehensive profile of stakeholders essential in building an effective communication plan for engaging and converting those charged with awarding the purchase or contract.

WHAT QUESTIONS CAN STAKEHOLDER MAPPING ANSWER?

"Who buys?" "Who cares?" "What matters?" Once again, these questions provide sellers with a simplified foundation or platform for discovery. In addition to these questions, stakeholder mapping further strengthens and guides the sales process by helping sellers answer a different set of six key questions. See Figure 1–1. Let's build out the stakeholder mapping platform and explore additional issues that mapping can answer.

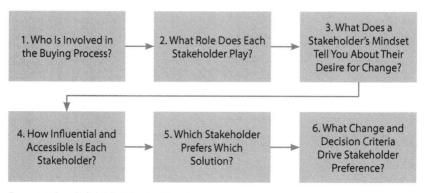

Figure 1-1 Core Stakeholder Mapping Questions

1. Who Is Involved in the Buying Process?

The primary goal of stakeholder mapping is to ensure that sellers survey the field of potential stakeholders, specialists, and parties with a vested interest. In a simple sale, there may be only one or two people involved. In a complex sale, there may be many people involved. Here are some recommendations for sellers.

Recommended Action

- In larger organizations, begin with organizational charts for each department, and ask, "Who has a responsibility, concern, expertise, or knowledge that might be relevant to the purchase of this product or service?" Think subordinates and not just supervisors, managers, and other management titles. Keep a list of all names and titles.

- Ask, "Have I overlooked any committees, groups, teams, or buying groups that might not show up on an organizational chart?" Consider oversight committees, value analysis committees, or new technology committees.
- Ask, "Are there any third-party influencers? Consider board members, consultants, advisors, industry peer groups, etc. They are often the invisible influencers.
- Ask, "Are there any new executive hires with an interest in the buying decision who have been excluded from the organizational chart?"
- Ask, "Are there any external participants?" Every time you have a sales call or meeting, ask for help in defining who is "internal" and who is "external." Be open-minded, but look to confirm involvement and participation.
- In a very large organization, you may wish to convert the list to "sticky" notes or to a whiteboard so you can easily move stakeholders from one classification to another as you gain information. Many CRMs will also let you map this important sales information visibly.
- Eventually you will have a list of all the internal and external stakeholders by name and title. See Figure 1–2.

Figure 1-2 Potential Internal and External Stakeholders

2. What Role Does Each Stakeholder Play in the Buying Process?

There are many sales methodology companies that have created helpful classifications of the roles or functions played by different stakeholders in the buying process. In the 1980's, Robert Miller and Stephen Heiman helped sellers understand four basic roles—Economic Buying Influence, User Buyer, Technical Buyer, and Coach.[3] The Rain Group identified five decision roles: Business Driver, Approver, Evaluator, Champion, and Domino.[4] Gartner outlines five different "buyers"—Business Buyer, Financial Buyer, Technical Buyer, Risk Buyer, and User Buyer.[5] Shonka and Kosch, authors of *Beyond Selling Value,* define contacts, decision makers, coaches, evaluators, and gatekeepers.[6] Bob Apollo of Inflexion-Point Strategy Partners describes a final approver, power sponsor, key contributor, gatekeeper, influencer, none, and uncertain categories.[7]

We encourage all sales professionals to find a methodology that helps distinguish buying interests and functions. If your company has standardized a specific approach, then use it. It's more important to execute a sound approach consistently than it is to have the "perfect" method applied inconsistently.

We offer the following framework of roles to illustrate the value of any method when combined with a mapping approach. Let's explore four key buying roles that stakeholders may play. See Figure 1–3.

Figure 1-3 Buying Roles/Functions

- **Executive Buyer.** This can be an individual, committee, or buying group—but he or she must have the ability to authorize the purchase and give the final "yes." Ask, "Who has the authority to say we are going with Firm A or to authorize an order with Firm A?" The Executive Buyer can be anyone in the organization who has the responsibility to authorize the purchase. This could be a Manager, Department Head, Vice President, CEO, Board of Directors, Principal Investigator on a grant, or Purchasing Agent.

  With committees, ask, "Who owns the initiative?" "Who created the committee?" "What is the committee mandate (to write a report, make a recommendation, select a final candidate, or make a choice)?" There is always, however well concealed, an Executive Buyer. The final "yes" may be a committee or buying group if it's a complex sale with several stakeholders with disparate needs. An executive may delegate authority if he/she wants consensus and buy-in from everyone involved.

- **User.** An individual that has the ultimate responsibility for the operation or use of the product, service, or solution and can be staff, supervisors, managers, or directors. Users (and there may be many on large buying teams) often view solutions in terms of performance and risk. "Will this solution improve our output or productivity?" "Will it reduce our costs?" "Will the selling organization customize the solution to meet our needs?" "What challenges will this change create for my staff?" "What is the seller's customer service record?" "What are the training requirements for my department?" "How will this solution impact my daily activities?"

- **Technical Advisor.** Technical Advisors often include representatives from Procurement, Accounting and Finance, Information Technology, Quality Assurance, Operations, Manufacturing, Compliance, Service, Human Resources, Board of Directors members, and Legal. This group can include consultants, third-party specialists, regulatory agents, and channel partners. Technical Advisors offer background, experience, and project knowledge, and they judge the technical and measurable aspects of your solutions. They may be charged with small tasks like writing an RFP or more broad-scale projects such as product testing. "Does this product meet or exceed our performance specifications?" "How durable is the product?"

- **Process Manager.** As buying teams grow in size and complexity, the need arises to have an individual manage the buying process, establish deadlines, communicate with vendors, share information with stakeholders, and govern the decision process. In large organizations, the Process Manager may come from Procurement and may be the lead on a project team, a consultant, or a political appointment. In other words, the Process Manager may also play the role of a User or Technical Advisor. In other situations, they will carry a separate and distinct role. The Process Manager will likely hold the answers to many questions surrounding committee composition, the "buying window," product specifications, financial support, and the decision process.

Why is it important to know which stakeholders serve and in what capacity? The answer lies in two key points: First, some stakeholders perform limited, highly contained functions like writing specifications, customizing the boilerplate on an RFP, or reviewing the contract language. They may not have a voting role, or they may have minimal influence. When pressed for time, the seller may find it necessary to overlook advisory stakeholders with non-voting or minimal influence, but for some circumstances, it will be imperative to include everyone. Second, individuals like Users, who perform the same or similar functions, tend to share a common vocabulary and similar interests and concerns. Technical Advisors will also share vocabulary, interests, and concerns with their focus on specifications for performance and cost.

Recommended Action

- Define the role that each individual plays in the sale.

- It's possible for an individual to play more than one role. For example, a stakeholder may serve as both an Executive Buyer and User or as both a User and Process Manager.
- An individual's title or department helps you uncover the role a stakeholder is likely to play. Encourage face-to-face conversations. They are the best method for understanding a stakeholder's function or role.
- Learn who the third-party influencers are, such as board members, consultants, advisors, or industry peer groups. They can have significant impact on buyers' preferences.

3. What Does Each Stakeholder's Mindset Reveal About Their Desire for Change?

A stakeholder's "mindset" is their perspective on the status quo and the need for change. "Why change?" and "Mindset" work in tandem to help you understand how well the status quo is meeting the stakeholder's desired business and personal outcomes. Mindsets reveal:

- Attitude toward the status quo such as anxiety over the current solution, curiosity about an alternative provider, or comfort with current arrangements.
- Perspective on how well the status quo is impacting business outcomes such as the current provider is exceeding expectations, underperforming, or performing inconsistently.
- View of change—helps the seller discover the buyer's inclination toward or resistance to change. Some buyers are open to change while others are reluctant.

Let's consider four mindsets and the insight each provides about the buyer. See Figure 1–4. The first two are receptive to change.

Threat-focused mindset. Buyers have a threat-focused mindset when they are challenged by a problem that is undermining business outcomes or is threatening impending negative results. In this mindset, buyers see the status quo as having failed or unable to address future challenges. They are committed to making a change. The key to selling to threat-focused buyers is to establish a clear link between your solution and the resolution of their problem and the attenuation of the impact that problem has on the business. These buyers are often driven by a strong sense of urgency and want you (the seller) to provide a roadmap for change and prove (data, research, testimonials) the capabilities of your product or solution. When faced with a threat, buyers are looking for an immediate solution to their problem.

Opportunity-focused mindset. Often buyers are faced with an opportunity to improve future business outcomes through increased revenue or profitability, improved client or customer retention, elevated speed of service, or enhanced product quality. Opportunity-focused buyers are open to change, but they want to make the change on their own schedule, and oftentimes this is in a new budget year. It's not "no" but "not today." While not committed to change immediately, these buyers are interested and curious about new solutions. If you are selling to opportunity-focused buyers, you will need to heighten their sense of urgency. Show how your product moves the buyer's business measurably forward in capturing the focal opportunity. Identify the "cost of inactivity" or delay. Make sure the buyer has a clear understanding of how your solution enables the buyer to capture the opportunity. The next two mindsets are more difficult selling targets.

Complacent Mindset. Complacent buyers lack motivation to change. Their attitude is one of contentment. They are satisfied with the direction of the business. Current business performance is viewed as adequate and "as expected." These buyers see change as an unwelcome risk in contrast to the status quo, which has known and measurable benefits. As a seller, you should focus on changing the buyer's perspective. Provide insight that changes the customer's view of the status quo. Ask yourself, "What is my buyer ignoring, denying, or avoiding that may alter their perspective?" Your challenge is to paint the picture that brings a future problem or opportunity into clear view for the buyer. Stories, examples, and testimonials can be helpful in changing the complacent mindset. You should use visuals or a whiteboard to show the "before and after."

Confident Mindset. Confident stakeholders are a seller's nightmare. They are resistant to change and committed to the status quo. They are confident in existing resources, suppliers, and products. There is no immediate problem, no impending threat, and no weakness in business indicators. Unless they are blindsided by a "trigger event," don't expect an easy sale. Some top performers develop a strategy that challenges the buyer's perspective. They develop an approach that combines education and provocation. Is there a story that helps you connect with the buyer on an emotional level? Remember: not all sales are winnable. There is a difference between a buyer who is a *prospect* and one who is a *project*.

	Buying Mindset		**Non-Buying Mindset**	
Mindset	Threat-Focused	Opportunity-Focused	Complacent	Confident
Attitude	Fearful, Anxious, Worried, Urgent, Despondent	Interested, Curious, Occasional Concern	Satisfied, Pleased, Content, Comfortable	Self-Reliant, Self-Assured, Euphoric
Business Outcome	Unexpected Negative Results, Underperforming, Impending Threat, Downturn	Improvement, Weakness and Soft Spots, Inconsistent Results	Adequate Performance, Meets Expectations	Exceeds Expectations, Positive Forecasts
View of Change	Committed to Change	Open to Change	Reluctant to Change	Resistant to Change

Figure 1-4 Types of Stakeholder Mindset

Change Drivers That Create Value

Clearly, some stakeholders want to maintain the status quo. They are not inclined to change unless you can identify a problem that must be addressed, an achievable opportunity with measurable upside, or a threat that must be contained. We call these motivations to change *Change Drivers*. A change driver is a force or condition that motivates buyers to seek change. There are three types of Change Drivers: Problems, Opportunities, and Threats (POT).

- **Problem:** An event, activity or situation that undermines business productivity. "Our customer churn rate is too high, and we must fix it immediately." The implications or results of an unaddressed problem are often clear to the buyer—loss of revenue resulting from increased customer churn.
- **Opportunity:** A change in business operations that would improve productivity or advance business goals. "We have developed some new technology that will radically change the way customers buy."
- **Threat:** A foreseeable difficulty or trouble that, unaddressed, could undermine business outcomes. "We have two new entrants in our market with products that are comparable to ours. We need to minimize their competitive impact and prevent customer defection."

Recommended Action

- Identify the value each stakeholder expects or desires to gain through change. Is their desire to solve a problem, pursue an opportunity, or vanquish a threat?
- Ask questions that will help you uncover their view of change. Are they committed, open, reluctant, or resistant?
- Determine what about the status quo—i.e., what assumptions the stakeholder is making about the current solution or supplier—drives value for the stakeholder.

4. How Influential & Accessible Is Each Stakeholder in the Buying Process?

Each stakeholder has a level of influence in the decision-making process. Their influence can be determined by attributes like their position in the organization, technical experience with the products under consideration, or by the organization's perception of them as thought leaders or change agents. But the most important determinant of influence in this case is one stakeholder's ability to alter or reinforce another stakeholder's preference. Think of "level of influence" as a "multiplier" that elevates the impact of a stakeholder's bias or preference for a product.

We categorize each stakeholder's influence in one of three ways.

- **Strong Influence**: Stakeholders whose voice carries weight with others and directly influences the decision of others.
- **Moderate Influence:** Stakeholders whose opinion is viewed as one that should be considered by the other stakeholders.
- **Weak Influence:** Stakeholders whose opinion has little or no impact on the perspective of other stakeholders.

It's often difficult for sellers to have access to all the stakeholders. While access can be extremely important in executing a sales plan, accessibility may change as the result of one's calendar, emerging crises, important corporate events (like Board meetings and conferences), and personal commitments. Accessibility can be measured as follows:

- **High Access:** Stakeholders who are easily available by telephone or personal visit.
- **Moderate Access:** Stakeholders who are available to you with some delays and periods of limited access.
- **Low Access:** Stakeholders with whom there is little or no access or a long waiting period for an appointment.

Recommended Action

- Keep track of stakeholders' level of influence, which may change during the buying process as their expertise or passion for a solution surfaces or declines.
- Don't assume that someone who is new to the organization has a relatively low level of influence. Leave the worksheet space empty until you have more data.
- Don't mistake "involvement" for "influence." Just because someone is highly involved and an active participant, they may not necessarily have influence commensurate with their involvement.

- Look for individuals with a strong level of influence that supports your solution and are willing to let their voices be heard.
- Be aware that levels of influence can change by project.
- Determine the current level of accessibility for each stakeholder.
- Recognize that the level of accessibility can increase or decrease during the buying process. Some stakeholders may develop other higher priorities or wish to delegate their responsibility. Others may choose not to be involved until later in the process.
- Understand that some stakeholders may always be inaccessible to the seller. Develop a plan to understand their needs and gain their endorsement.

5. Which Stakeholders Prefer Which Solution?

As a part of the mapping process, it's vital to track and record each stakeholder's bias or preference for both your solution and for your primary competitor's. Biases may change over time as the result of sales activity and internal pressures.

- **Champion.** A Champion serves as a coach, advisor, sponsor, or advocate for the seller. Champions can be internal or external to the buying organization. They help the seller navigate the buying process, connect with stakeholders, and leverage their strengths in the face of competition. Champions want your solution and you to win. Consider them as more than allies—they are mobilizers and activists on your behalf.
- **Favors.** This individual mildly supports your solution but isn't completely sold. They need additional information, reassurance, and proof.
- **Neutral.** Someone who doesn't have an initial bias can be considered Neutral. They are not in favor of any of the competitive choices and prefer the status quo. However, their opinion may change over time as they acquire information.

- **Concerned.** This individual does not support the seller's solution. They need time to evaluate the risk and reward. They harbor concerns or fears that must be addressed before declaring their support. They require details and proof.
- **Adversary or Anti-Sponsor.** This stakeholder opposes the seller's position and serves as an advocate for a competitor. They overtly or covertly communicate that they want you out. An Overt Adversary openly tells you they don't favor your product, service, or solution. The Covert Adversary works in the background to discredit you, your offering, and/or your company. Always look for an Adversary or Anti-Sponsor.

Recommended Action

- When evaluating how a stakeholder views a top competitor, remember that the status quo can be a forceful competitor—your most powerful opponents are the stakeholders in favor of the status quo and in favor of "doing nothing." If you are not the incumbent supplier, be sure to ferret out undiscovered or unconnected stakeholders. Every voter has a potential winning or losing ballot.
- Don't assume that people who are polite or welcoming are supportive of your solution.
- Frame questions to uncover any biases, concerns, and aspirations.
- Determine if any stakeholder is averse or resistant to change and what they fear most in the change process.
- Ask your Champions to share what other stakeholders say positively or negatively about the value you offer.
- Arm your Champion or advocate with compelling arguments (data, test results, and references).
- As stakeholders move through the buying process, expect fewer stakeholders to be Neutral. When you encounter a "Neutral" stakeholder late in the process, they may be withholding their preference for another product or solution.

- Develop a list of actions that you can take to move anyone who is an Adversary or Concerned to Neutral—and move those who are currently Neutral or Favor your solution to Champions.

6. What Decision Criteria Drive Stakeholder Preference?

Each stakeholder envisions one or more measures that a solution must positively impact to warrant a change to the new product or solution. These key performance measures are often gauged at the organizational, department, and individual level. Some examples are:

- **Strategic**: achievement of vision, mission, and organizational goals
- **Financial:** profit, costs, revenue by region, etc.
- **Operational:** defects, open orders, efficiency, etc.
- **Personnel:** employee satisfaction, turnover rate, number of open positions, etc.
- **Technical:** product specifications, warranty, etc.
- **Contractual:** pricing, payment terms, etc.
- **Customer:** acquisition, satisfaction, net promoter scores, etc.

Some sellers will offer "soft" benefits such as ease of use or less training required. Others will resort to commonly used financial metrics such as Return on Investment (ROI), Net Present Value (NPV), Internal Rate of Return (IRR), or Payback. It's important for sellers to impact a metric that is meaningful for the individual.

Individual preferences are driven by needs, concerns, and personal wins and losses. They may take the form of a perceived threat, perceived loss, or opportunity.

Recommended Action

- Ask probing questions like, "How will you measure progress or change?"
- Has a "trigger event" made the stakeholders question the status quo? What metrics have been impacted?

- Probe to determine how each stakeholder hopes to measure change. What metrics quantify success?

Stakeholder Mapping Worksheet

Stakeholders	Role	Mindset and Urgency	Change Desired	Influence	Accessibility	Views Your Solution	Views Top Competitor	Decision Criteria

Figure 1-5 Stakeholder Mapping Worksheet

Benefits of Mapping Stakeholders

In complex selling situations with many different stakeholders, it's often helpful to create a visual "map" of the stakeholders, their titles, and their function. It's especially useful when selling to a buying group or a committee. Often an organizational chart with a reporting hierarchy can be misleading. A "map" that includes informal relationships can clarify alliances and coalitions. A visual map allows the seller to see who might be able to assist them in swaying opinion and who may be an obstacle to success.

A Stakeholder Mapping Worksheet as shown in Figure 1–5 is also helpful when selling to multiple buyers because it shows visual gaps in "what the seller needs to know" versus "what the seller knows." It provides the seller a quick snapshot of each stakeholder's profile, what matters most to them, and the decision criteria vital to their purchasing decision.

There is an adage in some sports (such as marksmanship, archery, and golf): "aim small—miss small." It means that when you focus on a very small target, your misses are more likely to be small. The Stakeholder Mapping Worksheet helps the seller develop precise focus.

For readers who wish to go beyond a worksheet and incorporate a comprehensive "strategy system" into a CRM, we suggest you consider Strategic Selling® from the Miller Heiman Group and the use of their Blue Sheet.[8]

The Stakeholder Mapping Worksheet is a tool for sellers to use in complex B2B sales opportunities. The greater the number of stakeholders, the more vital it becomes for sellers to track the answers to core questions. But a worksheet is more than a recording device—it helps the seller build an effective sales activity plan. Here are eight ways sellers will benefit from a Stakeholder Mapping Worksheet.

1. Sellers can create an effective communication plan by connecting stakeholders with value drivers.
2. Sellers can prioritize sales activities and quickly identify stakeholders who are not supportive of their solution and the benefits they wish to acquire.
3. In a team sale, it helps sellers brief their sales team.
4. Sellers can customize their content and messaging based upon what truly drives value for each stakeholder—instead of focusing on price.
5. As membership on the buying team changes, sellers have confidence that they have identified all stakeholders.
6. Sellers can identify political alliances and voting blocks.
7. Sellers can see where they stand in securing votes and building consensus.
8. Sellers can identify time and resource requirements as they traverse the buying process and communicate with stakeholders.

Key Points to Remember

1. Many opportunities have been lost because a stakeholder, unknown to the seller, provided input that undermined the seller's competitive position.
2. There are two over-riding reasons why sellers find it difficult to identify the key stakeholders in the buying process. First, the seller

never bothers to "map" the buying process in the target organization. Second, buying processes across industries are becoming more formal and complex—often controlled by committees and teams.

3. Stakeholder mapping is a process that identifies the key stakeholders and their role, i.e., the Executive Buyer, Users, Technical Advisors, and the Process Manager involved in the buying and decision process.

4. Sellers need to go well beyond the question "Who buys?" and expand the scope of their discovery process while they drill down and determine the function performed by each stakeholder in the buying process.

5. It's better to start with a larger group of potential stakeholders and narrow the target field than to begin with a small cadre and find that you missed an important buying influencer late in the process.

6. Sellers should identify the terminology and measures that are important to each stakeholder while gaining their support.

7. A stakeholder's mindset provides insight into how receptive they are to change.

YOUR COMMITMENT

What is the one thing you will commit to doing differently because of reading this chapter? Please share it here or on a separate sheet of paper.

ADDENDUM 1: STAKEHOLDER MAPPING WORKSHEET IN ACTION

The purpose of this addendum is to provide a sales story, a partially completed Stakeholder Worksheet, and a list of discoveries that may surface from the use of the worksheet.

Story: A Seller Faces a Manufacturing Challenge

A regional sales director (RSD), Kim, was cultivating relationships with a team of stakeholders who were exploring their options for hiring a supplier who would provide vital materials for their manufacturing enterprise. From Kim's initial contact with members of the buying organization, she made copious notes regarding each stakeholder. An initial phone conversation allowed her to identify five potential influencers:

- Amanda Gamez, Vice President for Plant Operations,
- Ray Campos, Director of Purchasing,
- Ahmed Juroo, Director of Product Production,
- Janice Whitten, Budget Director for Production, and
- Ari Chapman, Chief Software Engineer.

Kim's initial "read" was that Gamez was the Executive Buyer, Ray Campos was charged with driving the process (Process Manager), Ahmed Juroo might be a User or Technical Advisor or both, Janice Whitten was a Technical Advisor for financial issues, and Ari Chapman would serve as Technical Advisor given his background with their automated production system.

As Kim continued her meetings, she made a concerted effort to discover:

- the mindset of each stakeholder and their urgency for change,
- the level of influence each member appeared to hold,
- the degree of accessibility of each stakeholder,

- the bias or preference held by each stakeholder,
- which solution each stakeholder prefers, and
- the decision criteria.

As Kim reviewed her Stakeholder Worksheet, she decided she might benefit from an additional round of interviews with a focus on uncovering stakeholder support for the status quo, understanding each stakeholder's mindset and sense of urgency, and then gauging the support base for each competitor.

Consider Kim's sample worksheet in Figure 1–6.

Stakeholders	Role	Mindset and Urgency	Change Desired	Influence	Accessibility	Views Your Solution	Views Top Competitor	Decision Criteria
Amanda Gamez, VP Plant Operations Internal	Executive Buyer	Threat-focused; Urgent	System is costly; can be a drain on budgets and a threat to other initiatives Threat	Strong	High	Favors	Neutral	Customization to address problem; wants cost savings
Ray Campos, Director of Purchasing Internal	Process Manager	Opportunity-focused Next year	Wants a system that doesn't require repair Problem	Moderate	Moderate; Juggling two projects	Neutral	Neutral	Error-free system; emergency resources
Ahmed Juroo, Director of Product Production Internal	User and Technical Advisor	Opportunity-focused Not urgent but in next 9-12 months	Must be customized to his needs; easy repair Opportunity	Strong	High	Favors	Unknown	Total Cost of Ownership; speed of service response
Janice Whitten, Budget Director Internal	Technical Advisor	Complacent Reluctant to change	Must be a great financial deal to replace the status quo Uncertain	Weak	Moderate	Concerned	Concerned	Cost and customization of solution
Ari Chapman, Chief Software Engineer Internal	Technical Advisor	Complacent Resistant to change	Internal software team can handle the challenge None	Weak	Low	Concerned	Concerned	Functionality of customized software; overall cost

Figure 1-6: Stakeholder Mapping Worksheet Sample

Here are some revelations that surfaced from a careful review of the worksheet.

- Kim detected the beginning of a voting alliance between Gamez and Juroo; she learned that her sales activity must strengthen this support base by answering questions and providing proof of a link between her product and corporate initiatives.
- With two stakeholders Concerned, and one Neutral, the decision could well drift toward the status quo or be "stalled." Kim learned that she must build a game plan to sell against the status quo.
- Chapman and Whitten are Concerned with Kim's solution and her top competitor.
- Chapman and Whitten had different Decision Criteria. Kim needed to address Chapman's and Whitten's cost concern and Chapman's concern about the functionality of the customized software.
- The worksheet showed that Kim has failed to secure a Champion. She has to build strength in Gamez or Juroo and address Juroo's key decision criteria.
- Chapman, although weak in influence, was a supporter for bolstering the status quo.
- Kim learned of the need to help Gamez, Juroo, and Whitten see the cost problems of Chapman's plan to counteract his influence and desire to maintain the status quo.

ADDENDUM 2: STAKEHOLDER MAPPING CHECKLIST

These questions will guide you and help you create a profile for each stakeholder or buyer.

- ☐ Have you identified all the internal and external stakeholders involved in the buying process?
- ☐ Are the stakeholders committed to change either immediately or in the near term, or do they want to remain with the status quo?
- ☐ Who performs which role in the buying process?
- ☐ Who has the power to authorize this purchase?
- ☐ Once purchased, who has responsibility for overseeing the implementation, utilization, and evaluation of the product or solution?
- ☐ At the executive level, who is pushing the initiative behind the buying process?
- ☐ Who has the authority to stop or derail the buying process?
- ☐ Who shoulders the most risk if the solution does not perform as expected?
- ☐ Who will speak on the seller's behalf in meetings or conversations?
- ☐ Are third-party sources (either internal or external) involved in the buying process?
- ☐ Who is charged with validating performance claims or building a business case to compare products or solutions?
- ☐ Who controls suppliers' access to the buying-team members and the flow of communication?
- ☐ Who will keep you abreast of the buying process and changes in the decision dynamics?
- ☐ Among the stakeholders and buying-team members, who is aligned with whom?
- ☐ Who is promoting your competitor either overtly or covertly?
- ☐ Who is most likely to win the deal at this point in the buying process?
- ☐ What problems, threats, or opportunities are driving stakeholder support for a solution that could include your product or service?"
- ☐ What is the mindset of each stakeholder? Are they committed or open to change?

Chapter 2

Blocking & Tackling

Fundamentals of Buyer-Centered
Conversations

"The new sales conversation is no longer a Q and A between buyer and seller.
It is a conversation between business equals in productive collaboration."
Linda Richardson—Author of *Changing the Sales Conversation*

Mastering the sales call requires research, preparation, practice, and the refinement of conversational skills. There is no room for the rote product "pitch," glibness, or a well-trodden script. In this chapter, we focus on how to research and plan an effective sales call. Far too many sales professionals arrive unprepared and rely on their ability to improvise and adapt when conversations falter. Often these meetings result in the loss of a valuable opportunity, reduced credibility, and a disconnect between buyer and seller.

Consider for a moment the challenges facing an event planner in planning a sales call.

Story: The Event Planner

Y-Brand Technologies was planning a sales retreat for its highly successful domestic sales team. The four-day, three-night event was planned as a celebration for a quota-busting year.

A similar retreat held the prior year was a disaster. The logistics were horrible. Communication was sporadic and late. The team spent the following eleven months complaining about the event. When the complaints reached the CEO's attention, the Sales Vice President (Bill) knew he had to find a solution. The CEO told him to find a top-notch event planner who would "do it right."

The Vice President of Human Resources gave Bill the name of an event planner, Sharon from Berkshire Planning and Entertainment, whom he knew from his time at another company. Bill contacted Sharon, shared some basic information, and arranged a second, more in-depth telephone call a few days later.

The Event Planner's Objective

From her initial telephone call, Sharon created a list of the event's basic details: time, location, number of attendees, preferred activities, etc. To prepare for her second sales call, she conducted background research that brought to light five selling objectives:

1. Differentiate herself and Berkshire from the competition on one or more critical capabilities.
2. Educate Bill on the resources required to stage the event.
3. Create a heightened sense of urgency around selecting an event-planning team.
4. Understand Bill's comfort level with her projected event planning costs.
5. Gain a commitment from Bill to allow Sharon to act on his behalf to schedule rooms for the meeting dates.

Think about Sharon's plan. At the end of this chapter, we share some of the background research, insights, questions, and value Sharon planned for her second sales call.

> **Seller's Challenge:** *Research and Plan a Sales Call that Drives the Buying Process*
>
> The seller's challenge in planning an effective sales call is to build a strong foundation for action that will drive the buying process forward. Effective sales calls don't happen by accident—they require research and planning. Effective conversations are the building blocks of business relationships.

HARSH REALITIES OF THE SALES CALL

Have you ever noticed how we (as consumers) are drawn to the word "perfect?" It doesn't matter whether it's the perfect golf swing, the perfect facelift, or the perfect lawn—we are driven irrationally to discover the secret ingredient that makes one solution superior to all others. We want so much to believe in perfection that we buy golf clubs, books, dietary supplements, weed killer, and face cream to solve our imperfections. If you search for the "perfect sales call" on the internet, you'll find a trove of books, articles, and blogs. Most provide excellent insight and advice—none of them provide the elusive perfection gene. Why not? This is where reality sets in.

- **There is No "Perfect Sales Call."** Sorry, but you could see this one coming. There are just too many unknowns in the sales equation. 50% of every sales call may consist of unexpected events that any experienced seller can recite.
- **Adaptation Is More Important Than Perfection.** A vital key to the success of any sales call is knowing when and how to adapt to challenges, unexpected intrusions, and unpredictable responses from your prospective customer. Scripts just won't cut it. You've got to be able to think on your feet, listen carefully, and adapt to your buyer or stakeholder.

- **It's Not What Buyers Say—It's What They Do That Matters.** Buyers are nothing if not polite (not always, but most of the time). They nod their heads, smile, and voice their agreement. Agreement is not commitment. You'll need action from the buyer's side of the table if you want to win the sale. Each sales call should end with a commitment by one or more stakeholders that moves the buying process forward.
- **You Will Never Feel Comfortable in Someone Else's Skin.** There are lots of great role models. Watch, listen, and learn. But don't try to be someone else. Get comfortable with what works for you. The more you research and plan, the more comfortable you'll feel with your call plan and personal style.
- **The Illusion of Linearity.** Don't get hung up on linearity that says, "At step one you should do this, and at step two you should do that," etc. Your buyer will immediately sense something mechanical about the sales call. Instead, have a clear objective for the call—any roadmap that gets you there will be a good one.
- **Let Your Sales Funnel Be Your Guide.** Know your sales funnel, and make sure you know the direction you need to take the conversation, so it will move the buy-sell process forward. The sales funnel is the seller's best road map.
- **Some Sales Calls Reveal There Is "No Fit."** Most often this happens on initial sales calls, but it can also happen later in the buying process. You may be disappointed to learn that a hard-earned appointment only confirms that your solution is not a good fit for your prospect's need. Politely explain this to the stakeholder, recommend another supplier if applicable, and ask to be considered for future business. They will see you as a sales professional, and you will build credibility.

What Is a "Sales Call Plan?"

A call plan is an organized group of facts, observations, questions, and phrases that help the seller guide, probe, provide insight and information, and respond during the call. A sales call plan is NOT a script. It's a planning document for conducting a successful conversation.

> *"A sales call plan is an organized group of facts, observations, questions, and phrases that help the seller guide, probe, provide insight and information, and respond during the call."*

Many sales call plans are designed to be formulaic or sequential—a step-by-step process. These plans often introduce an element of confusion. Sales calls vary. They don't all have the same objective, occur at the same level in an organization, have the same number of participants, or last the same length of time. Think of a sales call method as a recipe you can alter to suit your taste (or situation). Keep your overall objective for the meeting in mind. Don't let a sudden change in the venue or sequence of events throw you off. While steps are not linear, some issues or topics are better addressed before others (for example, you cannot provide a solution until you understand the stakeholder's needs).

Instead of taking an "all or nothing" approach to the sales call, let's make a checklist of the primary elements that may help the seller choose, organize, and adapt to the participants, objectives, and time frame of the meeting.

PREPARE FOR THE SALES CALL: CORE ELEMENTS

The most valuable step a seller can take to ensure success is to control what is controllable. If you combine a bit of research with planning, you'll be amply rewarded! Not every sales call requires extensive preparation. In Figure 2–1 we've identified the basic ingredients of effective sales calls. Combine them to build your credibility.

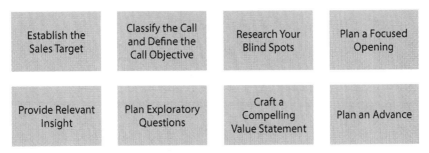

Figure 2-1 Core Elements

- **Establish the Sales Opportunity.** The purpose of the sales opportunity is to define what you hope to sell (product, service, or solution) to your prospect (company, division or department), the time frame (day, month, and year), and for how much revenue (prorated to the end of your fiscal year and also the annual revenue). The purpose of identifying your sales opportunity is to target and plan your sales activity based upon "to whom" you plan to sell, "what" you plan to sell, for "how much," and "when." All CRM systems will ask for this basic information.

  Recommended Action: Expect the ultimate sales target to change and evolve over time. Before the initial sales call, a seller may plan from pure conjecture until he/she can verify a need that can be addressed by the product or solution. However, by the end of the initial sales call, top performers have begun to consider a "go" or "no go" decision based on their ability to bring a problem, opportunity, or threat into focus for the buyer.

- **Classify the Call and Define the Call Objective.** There are six types of sales calls: Prospecting/Qualifying Calls (including cold calls and follow-ups to leads), Cross Selling Calls (the focus here is to sell other company products or services), Renewal Calls (the focus here is on retaining or extending an existing business relationship), Pursuit Calls (the focus here is on driving a defined sales opportunity), Presentations, and Closing Calls.

  A call objective defines what you need to learn from your prospect and what your prospect needs to learn from you.

  Recommended Action: Classify the call based upon your intent and what you believe is the intent of the prospect or buyer. By classifying the sales call, you begin to outline the research and planning required for a successful meeting. The ultimate sales target gives you a clear grasp of the future sales goal. Expect the ultimate sales target to change and evolve over time.

Then look closely at your sales funnel, and determine what you need to accomplish to qualify or move the sales opportunity forward. Ask yourself, "Where is the buyer in the buying process?" "What information do I need to acquire or confirm?" Answer the question, "What's in this meeting for the buyer?" Keep in mind your experience (or lack of experience) with this buyer and the time allocated for your meeting.

- **Research Your Blind Spots.** Even the most experienced seller has "blind spots" in their sales call preparation. Top performers admit their weaknesses and use available research tools to minimize their shortcomings. Here are some questions that top performers ask themselves to help overcome their blind spots:
    - Do I have a firm grasp on the competitive landscape?
    - How powerful is the status quo? Which stakeholders are likely to support the current supplier?
    - What are the documentable costs over time of "doing nothing"?
    - Where is the buyer (what phase?) in the buying process?
    - What is their "buying window" or timetable for a decision?
    - How are decisions made? Majority rule? Consensus? One person?
    - What is the problem, opportunity or threat and why now?

  Recommended Action: Probe for essential missing information by asking questions during the sales call. Use your time wisely.

- **Plan a Focused Opening.** A focused opening is a brief statement that communicates the purpose of the meeting and "What's in it for the buyer?" The purpose of the opening statement is two-fold: it sets an expectation for what the buyer will gain from the conversation, and it secures permission to ask some exploratory questions.

  Recommended Action: Identify two or three issues that concern or interest the customer or buyer. Verify the prospect's interest, and allow the buyer to add items to the agenda. "Since we spoke last week on the phone, have you thought of anything that you'd like to add to our agenda?" Remember, if there are any buyer issues that remain unaddressed, you may never have another chance to overcome them and gain traction.

- **Provide Relevant Insight.** Insight may arise from your observations or questions. You can share insight from a research finding, a lesson learned from another customer, or results from product testing. You can tell a short story or outline a "road map" on a white board. Be sure your insight is relevant to the buyer, memorable, and builds your credibility. Buyers want to know that you understand their industry. What can you offer that will pique their interest or provide a unique perspective?

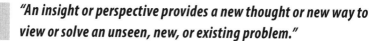

> *"An insight or perspective provides a new thought or new way to view or solve an unseen, new, or existing problem."*

What is an insight or perspective? It's a new thought or new way to view or solve an unseen, new, or existing problem. The goal of an insight is to get stakeholders to reconsider their current assumptions, beliefs, or judgments and open their eyes and ears to a new perspective.

Insights can be powerful. Here are some examples of what they can accomplish. They can:

- Create and appeal to a buyer's curiosity
- Challenge conventional wisdom and offer an alternative to the status quo
- Challenge a customer's thinking but not the customer
- Link to one or more of your strengths
- Increase your credibility when properly supported
- Create a contrast
- Elicit stakeholder feedback

It's important to get the stakeholder engaged early. Questions are still very relevant in a sales call, but they must be asked in the context of fixing or avoiding a business problem or capitalizing on an opportunity. Insights should guide the seller's questions.

Providing insight can be helpful in opening a buyer's eyes to an alternative view of their situation. But insight can drive an entirely different strategy or approach to the selling process. In Chapter 3 we explore how insight-driven conversations aid top performers.

Recommended Action: Consider the list above. How are you challenging conventional thinking? Is your challenge linked to one or more of your strengths? Is your observation or insight well supported? How will you elicit customer feedback and expand the conversation? Nothing is more detrimental to your success than an observation that seems disconnected or irrelevant.

- **Plan Exploratory Questions.** Based upon the sales call objective, craft several questions that will help you determine the relationship between the needs of the buying organization and the buying process. What benefits will the buyer gain from a purchase? Help the buyer identify and articulate the problem(s) and the implications of an unaddressed problem.

  Recommended Action: Focus your exploratory questions on what a customer wishes to correct (problem), achieve (opportunity), or avoid (threat). Help the buyer identify the personal and business implications of their current situation.

- **Craft a compelling value statement.** Using the buyer's terminology, state the unique and powerful benefits your product, service, or solution provides for the buying organization. How does your product help the buying organization mitigate a problem, eliminate a threat, or enable the buyer to achieve an opportunity? Be prepared to document your claim.

Recommended Action: Connect a compelling value statement about your product, service, or solution to the need or interest of the buying organization. Call a couple of your recent buyers and ask them, "What has our product helped you accomplish, and why is that important to you?" You'll be surprised at how quickly you'll find a way to express value.

- **Plan an Advance or request for action.** Consider your call objective and the positioning of this opportunity in the funnel. What's the next step? Be prepared to ask the buyer to take a reasonable step forward or "Advance" in the buying process. The buyer might schedule a presentation, introduce you to another buyer, or share relevant data. Your funnel should suggest "what's next." Also give thought to any reasonable step you can take that would help the buyer and warrant a subsequent meeting.

  An Advance should be tied to a timeline; otherwise it's an intention and not an action.

  Sample Advance questions: "Based on our conversation today, are you comfortable setting up a follow-up meeting with John, Fred, Mary Anne, and yourself for next Monday to discuss X, Y, and Z?"

  "If we get you the test results by Friday, can we schedule a follow-up call for next Wednesday to get your reaction to it and determine next steps?"

  Recommended Action: Look at your funnel and determine the one or two actions that will move this sales opportunity forward. An advance is focused on actions taken by both sides of the table. It must advance the buying process and the selling process. It's wise to have a primary and secondary commitment in mind. The primary commitment is more aggressive while the secondary is your "fall back" advance. During the meeting, the buyer's interest level and sense of urgency will help you determine which actions are more appropriate.

Story: The Event Planner (Conclusion)

At the beginning of this chapter, we shared the story of an event planner and her upcoming sales call. Below you will find four of her key objectives and a quick explanation of how she attempted to achieve her plan. How well did she do in applying the fundamentals of a buyer-centered conversation?

The Seller's Challenge

Sharon, an event planner for Berkshire Planning and Entertainment, planned for her upcoming sales call with the SVP from Y-Brand. She had an initial ten-minute call with Bill to determine the basics of their event: time, location, number of attendees, preferred activities, etc. Before her second sales call, Sharon reviewed the company's website and familiarized herself with their products. She read their annual report, reviewed their financials, and noticed that they were an extremely fast-growing and profitable company whose stock had risen 30% during the last year. She also read their recent postings on social media and reviews on Glassdoor and Yelp. Her research and the information gleaned from the previous call enabled her to formulate her sales target. When the time arrived for her second telephone sales call, Sharon had a clear call objective and knew what Advance she wanted Bill to agree to at the end of the call. Her research and planning allowed Sharon to accomplish the following:

1. Sharon differentiated herself and Berkshire from the competition on one or more critical capabilities while educating Bill on the resources required to stage a successful event.

   Sharon planned and interjected several points of information and education in the sales call:

   • Berkshire conducts pre- and post-event surveys to determine three factors: attendee's past experiences, attendee's on-site preferences, and attendee satisfaction. This enabled Sharon to assemble a program that ranks high with attendees and drives satisfaction. Berkshire's massive database provides their customers with a model for predicting participant choices among activities like golfing, fishing, sailing, beach activity, shopping, etc.

- With a large pool of part-time and contract employees, Berkshire can easily handle staffing needs for small and large meetings. This reduces the pressure on the client's staff and ensures backup while providing staff who know their function, the hotel, and transportation.

- Berkshire has extensive community contacts that allow them to arrange last-minute (indoor) activities when weather disrupts outdoor plans. ("For example, we recently arranged for several assistant coaches from the Miami Dolphins to provide a briefing on the different offensive and defensive schemes in the NFL. We took buses to the Dolphins training facility and got a tour as well. The group loved it! You aren't just contracting for plans—you're getting an insurance policy that guarantees success.")

- Berkshire's research can help Bill understand important differences in today's attendees: The demographic profile of Bill's team can predict preferences:
  - Attendees highly value a memorable event (like a briefing by Dolphin coaches) not duplicated at other events.
  - Interest in golf is losing ground rapidly.
  - Interest in fishing, sailing, and boat tours of the Everglades is increasing rapidly. In fact, interest in boating exceeds interest in golf.

2. Sharon created a heightened sense of urgency around selecting an event-planning team.

    Sharon conveyed the following in the sales call:

- Bill is facing deadlines on booking hotel rooms. Berkshire can act quickly to secure the needed rooms or explore high-quality options.
- She explained, "As you know, we are moving into our peak season. Hotels, golf courses, restaurants, and airlines get completely booked. I know some hotel executives who owe me a few favors, and I can get the ball rolling quickly."
- Berkshire can provide drafts of emails that can be sent to all attendees and guests to speed communication and establish expectations. Berkshire can help Bill create a comprehensive communication plan for coordinating attendees, guests, and corporate leadership by providing the right information at the right time.

3. Sharon tested Bill's comfort level with her projected event-planning costs.

   Sharon conveyed the following in the sales call:

- An initial draft budget based upon other events of Y-Brand's size with similar group activities. She asked, "Are you comfortable with a budget in this range?" "Have we missed anything in our discussion that would make this a better experience for the sales team?" "If you choose Berkshire, I'd like to take this week to work up a more precise budget based upon known events (like golfing, sailing, or deep-sea fishing), actual transportation costs, and local vendors."

4. Sharon gained a commitment from Bill that allowed her to act on his behalf to schedule rooms for the meeting dates.

   Sharon conveyed the following in the sales call:

- She shared a sample "letter of intent" that would provide her authorization to book rooms on behalf of Y-Brand. She also provided Bill a sample contract to complete with a list of initial timelines. "I know time is short—I can get you some answers before close of business today."

How Did Sharon Do?

- Did she have a clear sales target for the call?
- Did she have a call objective?
- Did she prepare for the call by conducting research?
- How did she engage Bill with a focused opening?
- How did she educate Bill or challenge his perspective with insight?
- Did she use exploratory questions?
- How did she differentiate herself and Berkshire?
- How did she create a sense of urgency?
- What action steps did she pose to drive the decision and advance the process?

Sales calls are as different as snowflakes or fingerprints. Forcing them into the same mold is hopeless. The best advice we can give you is to keep the interest of your customer at the center of all you ask and say. Respect your customer by showing that you are willing to spend a little time researching their background, their expertise, and their company. See Addendum 3 for Sources of Background Research. Respect your company and product by sharing your passion for what your product can do for the right customer.

Key Points to Remember

Prepare for your next sales call by considering these key points.

1. There is no "perfect" sales call. There are too many unknown and unpredictable factors.
2. Don't mislead yourself into thinking that every sales call should follow a step-by-step, linear sequence.

3. The best advice is to prepare thoroughly and know the customer, the company, the industry, and how other customers have benefited from your product or service.

4. Be sure you have a clear objective for the sales call—let that objective be your guide.

5. Plan to offer insight or ask probing questions that will engage your customer (and possibly challenge their perspective of the status quo).

6. Insight or perspective provides a new thought or new way to view or solve an unseen, new, or existing problem.

7. Share a compelling value statement that differentiates your product from the competition.

8. Close the sales call with an advance that secures a commitment from the stakeholder. The advance must move the buying process forward.

YOUR COMMITMENT

What is the one thing you will commit to doing differently because of reading this chapter? Please share it here or on a separate sheet of paper.

ADDENDUM 3: WHERE TO GO FOR BACKGROUND RESEARCH

Buyers and executives from a buying organization expect sellers to keep abreast of their organization's changes and challenges. What headwinds are the buyers and executives encountering? What opportunities preoccupy the executive level? What's new on the competitive landscape? What initiatives are planned to drive revenue growth?

A seller can readily access most of this information with a little research. Consider it *"table stakes."* Start with collecting information about the buying organization and industry. As a seller, it's difficult to be credible and effective if you fall short in your background knowledge. Your research will bring you up to speed on the company's business health, objectives for the year, product positioning, the climate of the market (soft or hard), and the industry's perceptions of the company.

- **Market Intelligence Sources**
  - D and B Hoover's
  - Inside View
  - Avention's OneStop
  - Gartner, Inc.
  - Forrester, Inc.
  - Google Alerts
  - Discover.org
  - Quora
  - Glassdoor
  - Associated Press
  - Routers News Agency
  - PR Newswire
  - Newspapers of the World
  - Wall Street Journal
  - Yahoo Finance
  - *The Economist*
  - AngelList
  - Datanyze
  - Value Line
  - Credit Bureaus
  - Standard and Poor's
  - U.S. Industrial Outlook
  - Office of the Secretary of State

- **Public Documents and Conversations**
    - Annual Reports
    - 10-K/10-Q Reports
    - 8-K Report
    - Proxy Reports
    - Quarterly Investor Calls
    - Public Speeches
    - Conference Papers
    - Press Releases and Announcements
    - Analyst Reports
    - Federal, Regional and Local Reports
- **Company Sponsored Events**
    - Executive Briefings
    - Webcasts and Presentations
- **Company Website**
    - Company Overview
    - Products and Services
    - Blog
    - Press, Media Page
    - Careers
    - Profiles of Key Executives
    - Board of Directors
- **Interviews**
    - With Direct Reports
    - With Consultants
    - With Channel Partners
    - With Contractors
- **Professional Networking**
    - Current Employees
    - Former Employees
    - Boards
    - Competitors
- **Industry Meetings**
    - Trade Shows
    - Conferences
    - Regional Events
    - Local Events
- **Social Media Presence**
    - LinkedIn and Twitter: Individual and Company
    - Facebook: Company and Individual
    - Instagram
    - YouTube Videos

- **Internal Information**
  - CRM Data
  - Marketing Automation
  - Industry Trade or Association Journals
  - Industry Blogs and Newsletters
  - Industry Reports
  - Competitive Press Coverage

Chapter 3

Selling to Resistant Buyers

The Power of Insight-Driven Conversations

"Insight Selling is the process of creating and winning sales opportunities, and driving change, with ideas that matter."

Mike Schultz and John Doerr, Co-Authors of *Insight Selling*

THE NEED FOR INSIGHT SELLING

The greatest obstacle to selling may be the clutter of assumptions, hearsay, and judgments rattling through a buyer's brain at the exact moment a seller is presenting a carefully reasoned, thoughtful solution for the buyer's product or service needs. Selling would be greatly simplified if all buyers began with a clean mental slate—no product knowledge, no performance assumptions, no three-year-old research findings.

Unfortunately, a seller often faces a selling situation akin to a baseball game that has progressed to the fourth or fifth inning before the seller even arrives at the ballpark. Buyers develop strong biases that challenge even the most eloquent, thoughtful, and engaging seller. Some buyers appear to be immovable and inflexible.

Where should a seller turn when they need a "game changer"? Give some thought to insight selling, an option that clears away the buyer's clutter and opens the buyer's mind to an alternative perspective. Use *insight* to engage, share, and collaborate with the buyer.

Insight selling goes by different names: The Rain Group calls it Insight Selling or Provocative-Based Selling. Richardson Sales Training calls it Selling with Insights, and the Corporate Executive Board (CEB) (now CEB-Gartner) refers to it as the Challenger Model. Cognitive psychology categorizes it as "cognitive reframing," and the Miller Heiman Group calls it Perspective Selling. Depending on the author, the content on the subject ranges from a theory of selling to a best practice that addresses a specific type of buyer.

Story: The Lady and a Dog

Jennifer sells Pet Friendly Pest Control Services. Her largest target customer, Veneer, has been using the services of a competitor, PestFree, for three years, and Veneer is satisfied. In fact, on Jennifer's last sales call, the owner told her, "We have no pests in our building so why would we want to change? Our current vendor is doing just fine."

The owner of Veneer, Bob, has a Labrador Retriever, Bentley, who freely runs throughout the office. The employees enjoy his presence and fawn over him. He gets plenty of attention! Once a month Pest-Free comes into Veneer to spray for pests. On that day, the Labrador Retriever cannot be in the office because the spray is not pet friendly. During one recent visit, Jennifer was told that Bob had to take his dog home because he forgot that Pest Free was going to spray that day.

Jennifer's firm has just released a colorless and odorless pet-friendly spray. She believes her firm can now win Veneer's business. Jennifer wants to provide insight for Bob via a voicemail or an email that will earn her an appointment with him.

Jennifer wanted to pique Bob's interest and recognize his concern for Bentley. Here are two options she considered:

- "Hello, Bob. I met Bentley today when I visited your office. In your absence, Bentley was in command. I know how important our dogs are to our whole family. Pest controls that aren't pet friendly can kill or cause severe damage to our pets' nervous systems. Further, veterinary treatments to correct the toxic and poisonous chemicals in traditional pest treatments can cost several thousand dollars. I have a plan that would keep Veneer's facility pest free and Bentley safe—and in total control of the office—in your absence, of course. Interested?" Voicemail.

- "Hello, Bob. I represent Pet Friendly Pest Control Services and provide commercial pest-control services to many businesses in your complex. I understand that you take your family's Labrador Retriever to work most days. Labs are great companions, but they trust their health and safety to us. Pest controls that aren't pet friendly can kill or cause severe damage to a pet's nervous system. The National Pet Care Organization (NPCO) reported that more than 11,000 dogs and cats were killed by exposure to toxic and poisonous substances last year. We can ease your fears, eliminate pests, and protect your Lab. Ask the officers and handlers at the Belleview Police Department's K-9 facility, located a couple of blocks away from Veneer. You can imagine how demanding they are of our ability to control pests and protect our K-9 officers—the 'furry kind.' If you would be interested in a secure and pet-friendly facility, I'd love to explain how our treatments protect and serve." Email.

How does each scenario include insight that may be relevant to Bob's interests and concerns? Does Jennifer provoke dialogue?

> **Seller's Challenge:** *When Faced with Buyers who are Strongly Committed to a Current Course of Action, Sellers Must Encourage their Buyers to Consider Alternative Options*
>
> Top performers draw from an arsenal of questions, test results, testimonials, and stories to pique buyer interest, share insight, and "reframe" the buyer's perspective of the problem and solution.

What Is Insight-Driven Selling?

In the book *Insight Selling*, the Rain Group identifies the three capabilities buyers attribute to winning sellers:

- They educate with new ideas and a different perspective on a situation that is relevant to the buyer.
- They collaborate and share.
- They present a strong case that they can achieve the results promised to the buyer.[1]

Richardson explains, "The use of insights at the right time and in the right way can truly help a seller to differentiate themselves, drive business outcome-based discussions, and create a sense of urgency in the buyer."[2]

Mike Kunkle, a well-respected author, states it this way: ". . . information or an idea that is based on credible research, authoritative content, or relevant experiences, which, when personalized to your client's likely or known challenges and opportunities and shared appropriately, opens your client's mind to think about their situation in a new way and shows them a path toward solving a challenge or capitalizing on opportunity through your company's capabilities and differentiators."[3]

Here's what insight-driven selling is not:

- A declarative statement that is surprising and challenging but not relevant to the buyer
- A tactic that shows how much more you know than the buyer
- A way to redirect the conversation to a topic that supports your position

Here's what insight-driven selling is:

- An approach that piques your buyer's curiosity
- A process of sharing insight and raising questions to promote collaborative discourse between you and your buyer
- A process of engagement that builds your credibility and secures the buyer's trust
- An exploratory process designed to educate the buyer
- A means of introducing a different, possibly new, perspective that questions traditional actions without challenging the buyer
- A combination of observations, data, stories, and experiences that will help the buyer "reframe" assumptions made about the status quo

The Language & Etiquette of Insight-Driven Selling

One of the most important elements of insight-driven selling is the use of etiquette, the language of collaboration, and shared discovery. Your language, terminology, and phrasing can create a "tone" to your dialogue that conveys shared learning and insight. This tone of collaboration and suggestion is designed to promote interest. Examples include:

> "I was surprised to learn that this solution is more powerful than I thought. . . ."
>
> "One of our best customers brought to my attention that. . . ."
>
> "I just read an article that I wanted to share with you. . . ."

When appropriate, use a third-party "voice" to share stories, concerns, and solutions. Don't lecture the buyer—share and collaborate.

> "I have a client who took a hard look at his current suppliers. We were both surprised at what he found . . ."
>
> "My client at XYZ has been on a crusade to avoid excessive inventory. We were brainstorming some options, and he came up with an idea that you may want to consider."

Use questions to raise options.

"What would happen if we tried _____ instead of _____?"

"How would _____ make things better?"

"Is this something that would interest you?"

THE SIX ELEMENTS OF INSIGHT-DRIVEN CONVERSATIONS

Insight-driven conversations are not linear or step-by-step sequences. In some instances, your conversation will require all the elements listed in Figure 3–1. Sometimes just two or three of these elements are necessary.

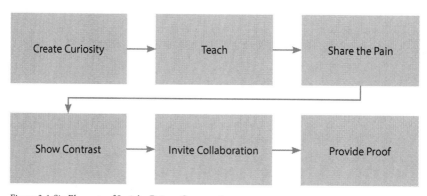

Figure 3-1 Six Elements of Insight-Driven Conversations

1. **Create Curiosity:** Begin with a statement that will resonate with the buyer and prompt their curiosity or interest.

2. **Teach:** Provide a perspective that states a business problem that concerns the buyer and matches one of your strengths. This is often tied to a problem they want fixed, an opportunity they would like to pursue, or a threat they would like to avoid.

3. **Share the Pain:** Highlight an unexpected risk. Show how it poses a threat to a positive business outcome for the organization or a personal problem for the buyer. Illustrate with a quick story, or quantify with data.

4. ***Show Contrast:*** Outline a plausible solution. Show a contrast between a buyer's current perspective and impending events by describing unconsidered needs. Illustrate how the status quo isn't as safe as originally perceived but there are remedies and precautions buyers can take.

5. ***Invite Collaboration:*** Ask a question to bring out the buyer's viewpoint. Encourage your buyer to outline a solution. You want a conversation, not a monologue.

6. ***Provide Proof:*** Provide proof of success. Offer evidence to support the claim that your solution will eliminate an underlying risk. Client stories add value and provide finite resources. They provide great evidence and help buyers see how other firms have successfully dealt with similar problems.

We'd like to share an example from our world of sales consulting and enablement that may help sellers understand how to position an insight—in a manner that will change the perspective of a stakeholder or prospect.

AN INSIGHT-DRIVEN SELLING EXAMPLE

As sellers, we continue to search for insights that drive a buyer to reconsider his or her perspective on a problem, opportunity, or threat. As consultants and sales-enablement professionals, we often find ourselves faced with prospects or buyers who have well-developed reasons for not investing in consulting services that can increase the productivity of their sales teams.

This is what we hear:

- "We made our number last year. Why would we want to change?"
- "We're an industry leader with excellent market share."
- "Our team has a lot of strong performers, and I trust them to solve their problems. The last thing I want to do is send the message that I don't have confidence in our sellers."
- "Ours is an 'up and down' business; while we missed last year, I expect us to be up this year."

Here's one way we deal with buyers' well-developed reasons for not investing in their frontline sales team.

Like most sellers, we run into our share of brick walls. We differ in the way we plan conversations to promote buyers' curiosity, share insight, promote collaboration, and surmount the brick walls. We expect resistance from our prospects and use their defenses to create a dialogue that (hopefully) will change their perspectives and increase their receptivity to change. As you read the following example, think of the brick walls you encounter, and consider how you can use your prospects' resistance to reframe a conversation and change their perspectives.

Here is our message in narrative form.

"Many sales organizations are deceiving themselves by believing that their sales funnel (their primary source for organic growth) is filled with winnable deals. The reality is the statistics show only 45% of deals are won, 32% are lost and 23% go to no decision or status quo.[4]

This means most sellers and sales teams are leaving millions of dollars in revenue and profit on the table. As a sales executive you know that, while it's tragic to miss your revenue goal, it's disastrous to not know you're headed for a miss until it's too late. The good news is there are ways to recapture revenue, profit, and market share, if you are interested.

Is it important to you to optimize the performance of your sales team? Are you looking for ways to maximize your profit and revenue? What if you could cut the revenue loss in half?

Through our work with medium- and large-cap companies in many industries, we have identified best practices that significantly reduce the 23% 'no decision' rate to 10% or less. As you might expect, we have client success stories to prove it. Would you like to hear some real-life turn around examples?

If you still feel these risks don't apply to your sales team, make a simple calculation. Recent research shows that the greater the number of buyers involved in making a purchasing decision, the greater the likelihood that the deal will result in 'no decision.' When there are 6 or more stakeholders, the probability of a 'no decision' increases to 69%.[5]

Calculate the revenue that you have at risk, and then let's talk about ways to lower the probability of stalled deals that undermine your sales quota."

Using the Elements of Insight-Driven Selling

In this section we have broken our message into the elements of insight-driven selling to illustrate how these components can be used to engage prospective customers in conversation.

- *Create Curiosity:* "Many sales organizations are deceiving themselves by believing that their sales funnel (their primary source for organic growth) is filled with winnable deals."
- *Teach:* "The reality is the statistics show only 45% of deals are won, 32% are lost and 23% go to no decision or status quo."
- *Share the Pain:* "This means that most sellers and sales teams are leaving millions of dollars in revenue and profit on the table."
- *Show Contrast:* "As a sales executive you know that, while it's tragic to miss your revenue goal, it's disastrous to not know you're headed for a miss until it's too late. The good news is there are ways to recapture revenue, profit, and market share, if you are interested."
- *Invite Collaboration:* "Is it important to you to optimize the performance of your sales team? Are you looking for ways to maximize your profit and revenue? What if you could cut the revenue loss in half?"
- *Provide Proof:* "Through our work with medium- and large-cap companies in many industries, we have identified best practices that significantly reduce the 23% 'no decision' rate to 10% or less. As you might expect, we have client success stories to prove it. Would you like to hear some real-life turn around examples?"

    "If you still feel these risks don't apply to your sales team, make a simple calculation. Recent research shows that the greater the number of buyers involved in making a purchasing decision, the greater the likelihood that the deal will result in 'no decision.' When there are 6 or more stakeholders, the probability of a 'no decision' increases to 69%.

*Calculate the revenue that you have at risk, and then let's talk about ways
to lower the probability of stalled deals that undermine your sales quota."*

When Provocation Works: The "When" & "How"

It's not unusual for sellers to encounter buyers who have adopted a defined
perspective on a problem or situation. Their perspective seems immutable
and inflexible. They have "screened out" any inconsistent information and
included only events, data, and experiences that support their perspective. What's a seller to do? Is it time to "cut and run?" Or, is it time to
become *disruptive*—to transition from educating the buyer to challenging
or provoking your prospect?

When your prospect is facing challenging and financially restrictive
options, it may be time for "tough love." Philip Lay provides a brief outline
of "when" to use provocation. "To begin a provocation-based sale, you
must do three things well: identify a problem that will resonate with a
line executive in the target organization; develop a provocative point of
view about the problem (one that links, naturally, to what your company
has to offer); and lodge that provocation with a decision-maker who can
take the implied action."[6]

So, when is it time to become disruptive and challenge a buyer? The
research team at Corporate Visions identifies several conditions that may
benefit from a provocative approach.[7]

1. **You need an approach that will capture the attention of buyers
   who have a strong commitment to the status quo.** Why insight?
   If you can identify an unaddressed concern, your buyers are less
   likely to screen out dissonant information regarding the status quo.
   You will create a new "thread" to the executive-level conversation.

2. **You know of a risk and potential failure of the current product
   or solution that your product can address.** Why insight? It undermines the buyer's perception that the status quo is without risk. If
   you can refocus the conversation on how the status quo undermines
   corporate initiatives, then you may have a winner.

3. **You have an executive-level buyer who controls the decision-making process, and you need to gain their support and sponsorship.** Why insight? If you challenge a perspective that exists at the executive level, you are more likely to redirect the course of discussion, and you are far more likely to gain immediate action.

4. **You must overcome the perception of your product as a commodity.** Why insight? Buyers can be very dismissive with value messages that (to their minds) overstate the benefits of a product. It will require a "sea change" in thought and discussion to reverse the current course of action.

Corporate Visions explains the "how" of crafting messages that challenge currently held perspectives. They cite research that points to three characteristics that will elevate the importance of a seller's message.[8]

1. **Your message should address an unconsidered need.** Why? It answers a vital question that undermines many sales efforts: why change? This is the vital key to driving the buyer away from the status quo.

2. **Focus on your product's unique strength**. This means crafting a message that illustrates the unique strength of your product in addressing the unconsidered need. Why? By connecting your product to an unaddressed and unconsidered need, it can create a true differentiator and demonstrate a benefit for the buying organization in a way that is not currently understood.

3. **Fuel the buyer's sense of urgency.** Why? You want action *now*. At the root of stalled and delayed sales opportunities is the failure of sellers to build a compelling case to change *now*.

But there is a final caution in Corporate Visions' research: "Challenging your buyer is the right approach *sometimes*, just not every time."[9]

Final Thoughts on Insight-Driven Selling

Insight-driven selling is particularly effective in opening a buyer's mind to an alternative perspective. Make a list of the concerns that your buyers use to challenge your claims. While test results, testimonials, and case studies can be useful, look for a fact or buyer observation that will provide an alternative perspective without challenging your buyer directly. You don't want a debate; you want an "aha moment" that changes the direction of your conversation.

Don't be misled. Developing a conversation around insight can be challenging. It requires research, planning, and adaptability. Quite frankly, it is harder than ever because a buyer's access to the internet means prospects are more informed than in the past. Look for the latest test results and customer surveys. The rationale for insight is not that it will surprise the buyer—rather, insight should help the buyer join the seller in carefully questioning and reframing the buyer's understanding of the current situation.

Last, scripts just don't work. A script will make your comments or questions seem stilted and mechanical. Give your prospect the opportunity to engage. Then adapt as you go. Be willing to change and modify your game plan. Make it customer-centric!

A sales call is a live performance. Your company, product, or service may have helped you get in the door, but the true measure of your effectiveness and value to the buyer will come from your preparation and demeanor, the questions you ask, and the perspective you provide. By raising one or more thought-provoking questions, you cause the buyer to pause and think, "That's a great question. I need to think about how I want to answer it." Thought-provoking, insightful questions create "aha moments" for the buyer.

Key Points to Remember

1. Make a list of informational points (test results, testimonials, case studies) and questions that are relevant to the buyers and may pique interest or expand conversation.

2. Choose an insight, or craft a probing question that will engage your customer (and possibly challenge their perspective of the status quo).

3. When using insight to drive a conversation, think first about what an insight is and is not. How will the insight change the dynamics of the conversation and the buyer-seller relationship?

4. Help the buyer "reframe" the perception of the status quo and the assumptions underlying the current bias.

5. Consider taking a more provocative approach when you are selling important new business, where there is a strong preference for the status quo, and when you are able to connect with an executive-level buyer.

6. For greatest impact, provocative or challenging messages should address an unrecognized need, focus on your product's unique strength, and fuel the buyer's sense of urgency.

──── YOUR COMMITMENT ────

What is the one thing you will commit to doing differently because of reading this chapter? Please share it here or on a separate sheet of paper.

_____

_____

_____

_____

Chapter 4

Road Blocks, Potholes, & Speed Bumps

Why Sales Calls Fail

"Structuring the sales call properly greatly enhances our chances of winning."
Mike Weinberg—Author of *New Sales. Simplified.*

Conversations are a bit like ballroom dancing. Both have a common cadence, direction, and mood. Like dancing, effective conversation depends upon choreography that coordinates partners. Who leads? Who follows? Where are we going? Each person's gestures and vocalizations can help forge a common bond or illustrate a lack of coordination. When the seller requests a conversation or meeting, he/she is faced with the challenge of coordinating the meeting in a way that connects with what is relevant, interesting, and valuable to the stakeholder.

Story: The Midwest Hospital Buyer

Many years ago, one of us was working in Marketing for a Medical Device Manufacturer and went into the field with a new sales representative on a routine sales call to gather some customer insights. The buyer was in a new role as a hospital director. He relocated from another region of the country and was unknown to the sales representative. Here is a reasonable recollection of the call—a disaster that only got worse.

Sales Rep   *"Hi Jim! Pleased to meet you, and welcome to Philadelphia! My name is Tony, and this is Tom. I'm your local sales rep from XYZ, and Tom is from our corporate office. He's riding with me today."*

Buyer   *"Nice to meet you both. How can I help you?"*

Sales Rep   *"Since you're new to the hospital, I thought I would explain how we have been supporting your institution over the last few years and acquaint you with our products. By the way, that's a great picture you have on the wall. Guess you like sailing, huh?"*

Buyer   *"Not really. I hate sailing. I hung it there to see how many sales reps try to break the ice with me by asking me if I like sailing. So far, I am 3 for 3."*

Sales Rep   *"Well, I guess I walked right into that one! Let me start over. As you know, your hospital made a major purchase of our technology for use in the ICU about 9 months ago. Are you familiar with our technology?"*

Buyer   *"I'm not familiar with your technology. At my previous institution, we used your competitor's equipment, and I liked it very much. In fact, I wish we had it here."*

Sales Rep   *"If you liked their technology, you will like ours even more. Let me tell you a bit about it—but before I do, let me suggest a format. Let's start with a detailed description of the specifications, and then I will show you a demo, followed by how to use the technology with four common clinical conditions. Then we can discuss our service and the warranty program."*

Buyer	*"Wow! Wait a minute. How long is this going to take?"*
Sales Rep	*"A thorough overview will take about 2 hours, but I can give you a broad overview in about 30 minutes."*
Buyer	*"Guys (looking at both of us), I don't have 30 minutes or 2 hours today. Why don't you make an appointment, and we can discuss this another day?"*
Sales Rep	*"No problem. That's a great idea. We'll do that."*
Buyer	*Before you go, what about this repair invoice I have for $1,500? I thought that's why you were here. I don't understand why we should be paying for repairs during the warranty period."*
Sales Rep	*"The cost was to replace a sensor that was damaged by someone during cleaning. It was an operator error."*
Buyer	*"It sounds to me like a design problem."*
Sales Rep	*"I can assure you the design is sound. Our service technician looked at the damage and talked to the individual who cleaned it, and they hadn't followed the instructions for cleaning."*
Buyer	*"Well, it certainly sounds like a lot of money to replace a sensor."*
Sales Rep	*"We certainly don't want you irritated with us. Why don't you let me see if I can't get that invoice amount reduced a bit?"*
Buyer	*"Good idea."*
Sales Rep	*"Thanks for your time today. I look forward to working with you."*
Buyer	*"Later."*

We have all been on a sales call that was like this one or worse. A sales call is a live performance, and you only get one take.

Seller's Challenge: *Conduct a Sales Call that Drives the Buying Process Forward*

The challenge in conducting an effective sales call is to overcome many of the obstacles that arise during the call, making sure to engage the customer, probe and listen to the customer's interests, adapt to the stakeholder's communication style, and manage their concerns.

This chapter will identify the stumbling blocks that can disrupt or derail the sales call. It will show you the steps the seller can take to manage the course of the conversation. All dance partners have missteps! The challenge is to re-connect and discover a common pace and direction.

TEN REASONS WHY SALES CALLS FAIL

No one intentionally tries to lose a sale. Even so, it's not uncommon for savvy sellers to inadvertently self-inflict a wound or two during the sales year. It's tough to be perfect all the time.

Whenever we meet with buyers, Procurement agents, and senior executives, we enjoy getting their feedback on "what works" and "what doesn't work" during a sales call. Here is our advice for the ten most common roadblocks sellers experience:

1. **Sellers fail to articulate a clear focus that resonates with the buyer.** The objective is unclear, and the conversation rambles from one point to the next with no discernible direction. It drives buyers crazy.

    Recommended Action: Craft a clear, focused statement. Guide the conversation by engaging the buyer about what matters to him or her. Remember "WIIFM"—all buyers will be asking themselves, "What's in it for me?" Without a clearly defined focus, a buyer will quickly lose interest.

2. **Sellers fail to manage time effectively.** Often sales calls take more time than the seller planned. Thirty minutes may seem like an adequate time frame, but if the buyer is running late from another meeting, your appointment may shrink to a few minutes.

Recommended Action: If events shorten or pre-empt part of the sales call, have a backup plan. You may recommend rescheduling for a future date. If you fail to gain a commitment for a subsequent call, you may forfeit your best opportunity to reconnect.

3. **Sellers talk too much.** Don't be a talking leaflet or brochure. Think about where the buyer is in their buying process, and then ask questions and provide information accordingly.

   Recommended Action: During the early stages of the buying process, the buyer should talk at least 80% of the time and then 50% of the time during the latter stages. Listen. Unless you can add value and insight, reserve your comments until the conversation reaches a point where you can link your product's benefits to the needs of the buying organization.

4. **Sellers make the meeting seem like an interrogation.** When sellers ask a series of "yes/no" or short answer questions, the buyer can feel pressed for answers. The mood of the conversation may seem combative to the buyer.

   Recommended Action: Give your buyer some "room to breathe." Sometimes you'll need to rephrase your question to give the buyer an opportunity to think about how best to answer. If you try to lead your partner, they will feel pressured to answer in a certain way. Always remember that sales calls should be conversations and not interrogations.

5. **Sellers use buzzwords that are misleading or artificial.** Don't exaggerate or embellish your claims. Don't use generic "marketing speak." Be specific to the needs of the buying organization.

   Recommended Action: Use terminology that has the same meaning for you and the buyer. Remember that words or phrases can mean different things to different people.

6. **Sellers fail to follow-up on a buyer's comment or contribution.** Don't skip from topic to topic hoping to land on an issue. Too many sellers ask a question and, upon hearing an answer from the buyer, fail to "drill down" and follow-up with a question. For example, the seller may ask the buyer to describe the problem, but forget to follow-up with a question that probes the causes, the implications, or the scope of the problem.

   Recommended Action: If a question seems to raise an issue on the buyer's radar, pursue the issue by asking follow-up questions. Probe the implications, size, scope and urgency of the problem or opportunity. Above all, use good listening practices. Once a seller understands the buyer's requirements, they can link their product, service, or solution.

7. **Sellers don't understand the buyer's business model.** Why does that matter? It can signal that the seller is unable to grasp the implication of problems and understand how the buyer's customers might benefit or be burdened by change. If the seller doesn't understand the business model, how can they help identify new revenue streams or unnecessary costs?

   Recommended Action: Explore how your buyer and his/her customers buy. Understand the steps they go through and the process they use to decide. What initiatives and new revenue streams are relevant to what you sell?

8. **Sellers fail to translate the conversation into action.** This one is a classic. You make a sales call, and it's going well. You feel the connection with the buyer. He/she is answering your questions, the conversation is flowing, and you are feeling great about the experience. Then something happens. Maybe it's a telephone call, an unexpected interruption by their assistant, or their sudden realization that they have another meeting. The sales call ends abruptly. They thank you for the meeting, and you realize you haven't asked for a commitment

or any form of action on the buyer's part. The opportunity to move the buy-sell process forward is lost, and you feel awful.

Recommended Action: Develop a call plan and stick to it. Resist the urge for exuberance when you sense the call going well. Stay with your plan, listen attentively, and be ready to ask for some form of action that will move the decision process forward.

9. **Sellers push product—not solutions.** There is an analogy that we use often in our sales workshops. We remind participants that "no one buys drills; they buy holes." You don't sell a product or service. You sell what a product or service does for a buyer or the buyer's organization. Stakeholders buy business outcomes.

   Recommended Action: Buyers don't spend money unless they see a return. The product you sell is simply a means to an end. It helps them eliminate a vexing problem, overcome a challenge, or capitalize on a market opportunity. Remember: buyers don't buy—they invest.

10. **Sellers fail to differentiate their product or solution**. All too often sellers focus on product features or vague qualities like "market leader" or "unmatched performance."

    Recommended Action: Focus on what your product does for the buyer or the buyer's organization. Show why market leadership is important? "In what ways is the performance superior and what will that mean for the customer?" Remember: most customers and influencers are well read and very familiar with your product and company.

Sales calls differ by industry, type of product, purchasing process, and even by geographic regions. We have direct sellers who sell commodities and sellers who sell enterprise solutions that cost millions of dollars. There are sellers in call centers who are prone to using scripts. A sales call can take place as the seller is qualifying the buyer, in the middle of the buying process, or while closing the deal. A call can drive account renewal or retention, or a new sale with strangers.

How Top Performers Manage & Elevate Their Sales Calls

One of the most compelling differences between top performers and their colleagues is the ability to adapt the sales call as the situation demands. Top performers have refined three skills: listening, using questions effectively, and the ability to manage the buyer's concerns as they surface. Let's drill down on each of these three skills in Figure 4–1.

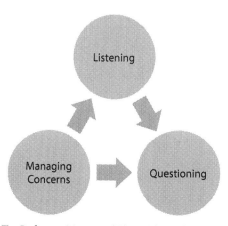

Figure 4-1 Three Ways Top Performers Manage and Elevate Their Sales Calls

We asked top performers how they energize and guide their sales calls. The following skills were deemed vital in ensuring a customer-centric conversation.

LISTENING: A SALES SKILL THAT IS OFTEN IGNORED

"Most people do not listen with the intent to understand; they listen with the intent to reply[1]." Conducting an effective sales call requires strong listening skills. Are you a great listener? How would your prospects rate your listening skills? Over the years, it's easy to lapse into complacency. You find yourself interrupting the prospect before he/she has completed their thought. As you know, it takes practice and awareness to listen attentively. Remember that the letters in "listen" also spell "silent." We should talk 20% of the time and listen 80%. It's how we obtain information, understand, and learn.

 "Most people do not listen with the intent to understand; they listen with the intent to reply."

What Is Listening?

Listening means receiving language (through the auditory channel), understanding the message conveyed and its importance to the speaker (cognitive processes), and then acknowledging the content through verbal and nonverbal cues. Listening is among the four essential language skills along with speaking, reading, and writing.

Listening is one of the most frequently used sales skills, yet it is the least mastered. It is fundamental and foundational—a skill that can help you develop or cause you to lose relationships and drive you to win or lose deals.

Three Types of Listening

Here is a quick refresher on the three types of listening.

1. **Selective Listening:** This is hearing only what we want to hear. We filter the speaker's content based upon our pre-existing assumptions and expectations. Our minds become a mental bunker that allows only certain words or phrases to enter. We hear select portions of the message and formulate our reply without waiting for the speaker to finish. If you find yourself taking a "mental vacation" while listening, you are using selective listening. The downfall is that you often miss key pieces of relevant information.

2. **Responsive Listening:** We listen closely for intent and context. We encourage the speaker to keep talking. Often the listener will

nod their head in agreement or use phrases such as "I understand," "Please tell me more," or "Please elaborate."

3. **Reflective Listening:** Reflective listening means repeating back parts of a message to confirm mutual understanding. It assures the speaker that he or she has been understood. For example, a reflective listener may say, "I want to make sure I understand you correctly. You are looking for a solution that is easy for your staff, takes the same or a reduced footprint on the bench, and can process a minimum of X tests per day with an uptime of 95% at or below $25,000. Is that correct?"

Eight Tips to Enhance Your Listening Skills

Consider enhancing your listening skills and improving your sales-call skills with a few simple reminders.

1. **Stop Talking**
   You cannot talk and listen at the same time. Mark Twain said it best: "If we were supposed to talk more than we listen, we would have two tongues and one ear.'"

2. **Pay Attention and Make Eye Contact**
   Give the speaker your undivided attention. Avoid distractions of any kind. You cannot listen attentively if you are focused on other people, sounds, etc.

3. **Defer Judgment**
   Listen to learn. Do not begin to craft a response or assemble a rebuttal in your mind. Instead, listen for the nugget that provides you critical information.

4. **Demonstrate that You Are Listening**
   Nod your head occasionally, smile, and encourage the speaker to keep talking by uttering phrases such as "Tell me more," or "Can you elaborate on that thought?" Keep your posture open and inviting. You are there to learn and then to speak only when it is appropriate.

5. **Pay Attention to Non-Verbal Cues**

   Whether you are on the telephone or face-to-face, nonverbal cues are always present. On the telephone, listen for cadence, tone, and voice inflections. When face-to-face, watch for boredom, enthusiasm, or irritation. This can be detected by the words used, facial expressions, and body posture. Peter Drucker said it best: "The most important thing in communication is hearing what isn't said.[3]"

6. **Ask Questions for Clarification**

   Ask questions to clarify what you have heard and to ensure understanding. Questions demonstrate that you are engaged with the speaker.

7. **Be Patient**

   Some people respond quickly—others require time to understand what you have said. They need time to compose a response to your question before they can answer you. Long pauses should not be interrupted. Give the speaker time to think.

8. **Provide Feedback**

   All of us have personal filters that often block or distort what we hear. Use reflective listening to paraphrase and repeat back what you think you have heard. Feel free to periodically summarize key points. This ensures comprehension and understanding.

In an often-repeated psychological study, researchers explored the relationship between how much someone talks (speaking time versus listening time) and how favorably they rate the conversation. Researchers consistently found a strong positive correlation between speaking time, how favorably they viewed their partner, and how much they enjoyed the conversation. Said another way, the more your partner or customer speaks, the higher they will rate you and their experience with you.

It takes concentration, practice, and determination to be a good listener. Listening is an acquired skill. If you are a great listener, keep up the good work! If you need improvement, follow these 8 tips. Good listening skills will improve your productivity and develop better customer and personal relationships.

QUESTIONING: IT'S ALL ABOUT USING QUESTIONS EFFECTIVELY

In any sales call, the seller should plan tactically to engage the buyer or stakeholder. Encourage the buyer to be an active participate in a "problem solving" or "planning" discussion. Effective questions can transition the buyer from observer to participant. Top-performing sellers know that questions should:

- Uncover needs or concerns
- Quantify problems
- Reveal predispositions
- Suggest an alternative perspective
- Prioritize options
- Share feelings
- Confirm an agenda or timelines
- Address points of discomfort, fear, or concern
- Test or validate assumptions
- Suggest next steps to move the sale forward

As you prepare, craft questions that will engage, reveal, prioritize, or explain. Think of your questions along the continuum of good, better, and best.

Often, sellers think they are asking great questions when they are really asking "good" or "better" questions. Take time to think through each question, and revise the wording to achieve the "best" impact.

- A *Good* question may uncover some basic information. For example, "Are you the individual who will approve the final purchase order (PO)?" The buyer's response is likely to be a simple "Yes" or "No."
- A *Better* question is "Who besides you will approve the final PO?" This response will provide some additional useful information because it tells the seller who else is involved in the final approval.

- A *Best* question might be, "Would you please walk me through the process to gain approval for a purchase order?" The answer to this question gives you their process for reviewing and approving the release of a PO or contract and who can provide the final "Yes." A "best" question provides you with the information you are looking for without the need to ask a follow-up question.

To be a top-performing seller, it's not enough to have a good strategy to win new business. Sellers must be able to execute effectively on every sales call. Your questions will build your image with others and provide valuable information.

Developing & Asking Questions

Preparing great questions helps you direct your thinking and shape the conversation to uncover the buyer's needs. Consider these key points when crafting and using effective questions:

- Great questions energize the conversation and make the buyer think carefully and thoughtfully before they offer a point of view.
- Highly productive sellers develop 4–6 great questions that arise from their research on industry trends, the buying organization, or the buyer.
- Great questions help uncover vital business interests, scope or size, the threat or opportunity, and they will identify essential benefits for the buyer.
- Great questions can politely and professionally challenge the buyer's perception of their circumstances.
- All sellers control the questions they ask. It's their most powerful sales tool! It's what sets them apart from all other sellers. It distinguishes them as memorable or forgettable.
- If you don't ask insightful and thought-provoking questions, you have lost the opportunity to engage the buyer in a process that can change how they think about the status quo.

- Great questions help the buyer define the cost of doing nothing and the payoff your product or service could provide them and their organization.

How Top Performers Use Questions

1. **Focus on the Buyer:** Great questions focus on the buyer's objectives, not what the seller wishes to sell.

2. **Plan a Conversation, Not an Interrogation:** Buyers don't want to be asked rapid-fire questions. Don't present questions like a checklist. The most successful sales calls are ones that are comfortable and conversational for the buyer. They lead to an open exchange of information.

3. **Listen Actively:** Great questions protect the seller from acting like a talking leaflet, and they remind the seller to listen!

4. **Ask One Question at a Time—Not Two:** If it takes two questions to get the answers, ask two separate questions. Buyers don't like answering two questions simultaneously. For example, avoid questions like, "Are you happy with your current vendor, and how long is the contract?"

5. **Dig Deeper:** There is a natural tendency to stop asking questions after you have heard a problem you can solve. Resist that tendency and ask several more follow-up questions. We use the analogy of digging a hole with a shovel. You don't stop digging until the hole is big enough. Dig deeper. Here's an example of digging deeper: "Ease of use is important to us." Resist the urge to explain how your product makes it easy for them to use. Instead ask a few follow-up questions such as "Explain to me why ease of use is important." "Describe for me how you measure ease of use." "Tell me what problems you encounter when ease of use is less than desired."

6. **Ask for Coaching.** A request for coaching changes the conversation from an interrogation to collaboration. For example, "I want to make sure that the solution we design is customized to your exact needs. Can you coach me on the key deliverables you are expecting?"

7. **Educate:** Design your questions to help the buyer understand their circumstances in a new light. An example is, "If you were able to save X dollars per unit, what would your company do with the savings?" or "How would saving X dollars per unit help you personally?"

8. **End the Call by Asking for Action:** If you don't end with a measurable next step, you have made a visit and not a sales call. The action that the buyer commits to take should justify your investment of time and resources.

Developing great questions takes practice and preparation. Consider developing a reference list of questions. You can select the best and most relevant ones for your upcoming call. Then role-play the call with an observer. The feedback you receive will be informational and unbiased. Remember the words of Albert Einstein: "It's not that I am so smart, but I stay with the questions longer." [4]

MANAGING THE CONVERSATION: HANDLING CUSTOMER CONCERNS

Concerns: Friend or Foe?

A sales concern (sometimes referred to as an objection) is an expression by a stakeholder about a barrier that exists between what they want and need before they will do business with you. A sales concern may take one of several forms. Consider these possibilities:

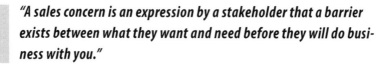

> *"A sales concern is an expression by a stakeholder that a barrier exists between what they want and need before they will do business with you."*

- **Timing**—Sometimes a buyer will suggest timing that amounts to a stall or postponement.
- **Price**—A buyer may require an unreasonable or unacceptable discount.
- **Politics**—A buyer may raise political issues to cloud and delay the purchase.
- **Misunderstanding or confusion**—The buyer may raise concerns over the capabilities or value of a product.
- **Suspicion, doubt, or skepticism**—The buyer may challenge the reliability or performance of the product.
- **Perception of risk**—The buyer may question your credibility because of a fear of being blamed for the selection of an unknown or unproven product.
- **Complaint**—The buyer voices a concern related to past performance.

Consider the seven types of buyer concerns in Figure 4–2 below and the corresponding approaches top performers take to resolve or address the issue.

How Top Performers Handle Buyer Concerns

Types of Buyer Concern	How Sellers Handle the Concern
Timing: • Buyer thinks the decision can be postponed • Buyer doesn't believe change is required today • Example: Buyer isn't convinced of the need for change.	**Create Urgency:** Demonstrate the cost of inaction.
Price: • Buyer won't pay the price quoted • Buyer thinks they can't afford the expense • Buyer wants a discount • Example: Buyer doubts the price value.	**Educate and Sell the Measurable Value:** Sell the ROI, NPV, IRR, Payback, Total Cost of Ownership or other metrics that are important to them.
Politics: • Buyer aligns with people not because they believe in the solution but because they provide personal gain • Buyers serve their own interests • Example: Buyer doesn't want to be personally impacted by supporting you, your product, or your solution.	**Devise a Personal Win:** Understand the political issues at play in this situation. Devise a personal win for the buyer such as recognition, promotion, reward, etc.

Types of Buyer Concern	How Sellers Handle the Concern
Misunderstanding or Confusion: • Buyer misperceives or is unclear about the product, service, or a contract provision • Buyer may be confused • Example: Buyer expects immediate delivery upon execution of contract, or buyer thought something was included that is not.	**Explain and Clarify:** Identify the point of misunderstanding; resolve the misconception through explanation and dialogue.
Suspicion, Doubt, or Skepticism: • Buyer questions the accuracy or veracity of a seller's claim • Buyer is skeptical and requires proof • Example: Buyer doubts the reliability of a new, unfamiliar product.	**Document and Prove:** Give solid evidence such as examples, case studies, references from consultants, users, or test results.
Perception of Risk: • Buyer perceives an unresolved risk or obstacle • Buyer sees a future downside that the seller has not recognized or addressed • Example: As the buyer's organization grows, changes will have to be made to the software, but no one is talking about time or the cost of growth.	**Mitigate Risk:** Demonstrate how the proposed product or solution is superior to the current solution; share "cost of inactivity"; look at long-term versus immediate gain. Provide references or testimonials from customers who had similar concerns.
Complaint: • Buyer has experienced a problem or difficulty in working with the seller or seller's company in the past. • Example: Buyer experienced slow response to equipment-repair issues over the last year.	**Demonstrate Corrective Action:** Demonstrate responsiveness with a plan to address the complaint.

Figure 4-2 How Top Performers Handle Buyer Concerns

LAIRE: HANDLING BUYER CONCERNS

It's one challenge to identify different types of buyer concerns, but it's an equally complex challenge to address and resolve these concerns when they surface during a conversation. Let's discuss handling sales concerns. Notice that we have said "handling the concern" and not "overcoming the concern." It's a subtle difference in wording, but the distinction is important. You cannot overcome a concern because the word "overcome" means "to get the better of" in a struggle or conflict. It implies that one conquers or defeats the enemy.[5] Your prospects and customers are not the enemy. If you argue with a prospect or customer, you can win the argument, but they will win the war. They will buy from someone else.

If you plan your sales calls properly, conduct great discovery by asking thought-provoking questions, and provide insight or perspective, you will reduce the number of concerns that surface. Can you prevent all concerns? Unlikely. But you can create an atmosphere that is less conducive to concerns.

Let's look at a mnemonic in Figure 4–3 to help you. The formula is called LAIRE. It stands for the following:

Figure 4-3 LAIRE Mnemonic

- **Listen:** Resist the tendency to answer a concern immediately or to become defensive. Instead listen attentively to thoroughly understand the concern. Demonstrate empathy to reduce resistance. Take notes if it helps you.
- **Acknowledge:** Say something to show that you heard what was said. For example: "I understand your concern, comment, frustration, etc." It is important that you acknowledge and not agree. At this point, you are not agreeing with them, but you are acknowledging their point of view.
- **Investigate:** Ask permission to raise questions that aid in understanding vital issues. Then ask a question or several. Seek to clarify your understanding of what you have heard. Don't assume you have an understanding; ask a question to verify it. You can't effectively answer a concern unless you thoroughly understand it. Example: "What exactly did you mean?" "Can you elaborate a bit more on the importance of that point to you and the organization?" It's also very important at this stage to ensure there is only one concern. Always ask, "Is there anything else that concerns you?"
- **Reframe:** The purpose of the reframe is to verify that you understand the concern correctly. Example: "So am I understanding you correctly that you want XXX?"

- **Educate and Confirm:** This is where you provide your response to the concern in a rational and unemotional manner and confirm that your response handles their concern. If it does not handle the concern, then you will need to restart the process until a positive resolution has been achieved. If proof exists, use it. Proof can be a reference, testimonial, case study, financial document, etc. Example: "Many of our clients have expressed a similar concern. One thing to consider is that . . ."

Let's look at the **LAIRE** process with an example.

Listen

Buyer: *"I don't think we can afford to spend that much money right now."*

Seller: *Listens attentively.*

Acknowledge

Seller: *"I can understand why you could feel that way. Our product does require a significant financial investment."*

Buyer: *"I'm glad to hear you understand my predicament. It's a lot of money."*

Investigate

Seller: *"When you mentioned that you didn't think the organization could spend that much money right now, what exactly did you mean?"*

Buyer: *"This month we have already had a rash of unusual and unexpected expenses. I think we will be over our expense budget for this month, and that's unacceptable."*

Seller: *"What happens when you run over budget for the month?"*

Buyer: *"We get reprimanded and reminded that our yearly performance bonus is at risk. As you can appreciate, neither of these are acceptable to us."*

Reframe

Seller: *"So, if I understand you correctly, the issue is one of timing for the purchase; it's not that you don't see the value our solution will provide. Is that correct?"*

Buyer: *"Yes, that's correct. The timing is awful right now."*

Seller: *"Do you have any other concerns other than the timing for the expenditure?"*

Buyer: *"No. But a price reduction is always welcome."*

Educate/Confirm

Seller: *"What if we sold you the product today at the quoted price and extended our payment terms to net 90 days instead of net 30 days? This would give you an immediate cost savings and would reduce your monthly expenses against your budget. It may not offset all the unusual and unexpected costs you incurred this month, but it would help. The extra payment time in effect gives you a price discount. Would that handle your concern?"*

Buyer: *"I can see the benefit to us with that approach. If you can give us 120 days payment terms, we can do the deal."*

Seller: *"I think that's a resolution that works for both of us."*

Is it always this easy? No, but the process does work. Sometimes you will not be able to handle the concern. In that case, you must ask for some type of commitment to keep the deal alive.

In the above example, the seller could have said, "I am not authorized to extend payment terms beyond 90 days. Can I have 24 hours to talk to my manager? If my manager approves the terms, can we meet tomorrow to sign the contract?"

It's always a best practice for sales organizations to identify all the most common concerns, develop a concern-handling process and then role-play the scenarios. This provides the sales team with the training and confidence to effectively handle any concern.

Key Points to Remember

1. Sales calls fail for many reasons, but the primary cause is that sellers fail to focus on the needs of the customer.
2. There are three types of listening: selective, responsive and reflective.
3. Effective sales calls require active listening skills on the part of the seller.
4. Asking insightful and thought-provoking questions can help the seller engage the stakeholder and discover vital interests.
5. There are seven types of buyer concerns: timing, price, politics, misunderstanding or doubt, suspicion, doubt or skepticism, perception of risk and complaints.
6. Any sales call can be disrupted by concerns raised by the stakeholder. Top performers prepare for concerns in advance of the call.
7. LAIRE is a mnemonic device that can aid the seller when unexpected concerns arise.

YOUR COMMITMENT

What is the one thing you will commit to doing differently because of reading this chapter? Please share it here or on a separate sheet of paper.

_____

_____

_____

_____

Chapter 5

From Gatekeeper & Blocker to Mapmaker & Guide

"The gatekeepers—receptionists, administrative assistants, and executive admins—field calls for the decision-maker. They're valuable to the executive, but not to you—not until you've developed your relationship."

Joanne Black—Author of *No More Cold Calling*

We all know that you can't sell if you can't get in front of the people who would find value in your product or service. It's a vital step in the sales process, and few of your other selling skills matter if you can't use them to engage buyers that influence, authorize, and pay for your product or service.

The challenge is that senior buyers are supported and insulated by tiers of executive assistants, administrators, office staff, and project managers, leaving the seller to question, "How will I ever get past the gatekeeper(s)?"

Several years ago, a colleague shared this story—an illustration of the changing role of the gatekeeper.

Story: The Power Behind the Throne

Carol, a friend for many years, had just taken a sales position with a company that sold office systems, equipment, and furniture. She was attracted to the position because the company sold more than $20M to the federal government each year, and her primary responsibility was to serve as "point person" for federal sales.

Carol was only a few weeks into her new position when she received notice of a bid meeting that was planned to determine the scope of work required to furnish new offices for a recently expanded government agency. She shot off a quick note to her boss and an email confirmation to the executive assistant named in the correspondence.

Two weeks later Carol, an equipment specialist, and a construction manager from the company attended the meeting. It included representatives from three of Carol's competitors—all well-known in the market. This was going to be a tough sale. She would be starting from scratch, with strong competition and a quick turnaround. She knew that getting to the executive buyer was critical, and time was short.

When the meeting was over, Carol and her two colleagues convened at a nearby coffee shop to share their observations and develop a sales plan. "Obviously, you're going to have to get to the executive buyer, or we're dead," offered the equipment specialist. The construction manager explained, "This is going to be a little tricky, given their security requirements. There's a lot of work and very little time."

Carol was quiet for a moment and then asked, "What role do you see the executive assistant playing?" "What do you mean? She's an administrative assistant!" remarked the construction manager.

Carol explained, "I noticed that every time there was a question that the executive couldn't answer, he turned to his assistant. Sometimes she would write a quick note and angle it, so he could read it. It seems like his assistant has a bigger role than was apparent."

After her two colleagues departed, Carol picked up the phone and called the executive assistant. Carol empathized with the challenge of putting together answers to questions from four companies on quick notice, and she offered her help. To give the executive assistant a quick start, she said she could put together a "boiler plate" on Q&A from other bid processes. Carol also offered a "scorecard" that had helped other agencies assemble buyer comparisons.

Over the next three weeks, Carol discovered that the executive assistant was taking a much larger role in the decision process than anticipated. She wasn't just the "admin." She was the project manager charged with developing a plan that included all construction, furnishing, equipment, relocation, security, and budget management.

Carol cultivated her relationship with the assistant through numerous phone calls, meetings, and emails—and transformed the assistant's position from gatekeeper to colleague. Carol learned that the assistant was charged with the responsibility to meet all project timelines, deadlines, and budgets whenever a department was faced with expansion, relocation, or reorganization. The assistant helped Carol build "road maps" and provided guidance during the selling process.

In today's organizational life, things are not always as they appear to be. Blockers may turn into "enablers." Gatekeepers may become guides and mapmakers.

Seller's Challenge: *Use the Gatekeeper to Access and Influence the Executive Buyer*

Discover a way to access stakeholders and decision-makers by developing strong relationships with potential blockers and gatekeepers. The most frequently mentioned sales challenge is discovering a pathway that allows the seller to connect with the executive buyer. Often gatekeepers block or misdirect the seller's efforts until it is too late in the sales process to positively impact the sale.

This chapter will explore the "brave new world" of gatekeepers. It includes some harsh realities of getting past gatekeepers: unlocking the mind of the gatekeeper, fatal mistakes in working with gatekeepers, and tools for accessing executive buyers.

YOU'RE SELLING IN A GATEKEEPER'S WORLD

So much has changed about the buyer's role and how we sell in response to their changing roles. Set aside the image of an administrative assistant blocking the doorway leading to the C-suite. Gatekeepers are no longer "stepping stones" to the executive level. Many of these men and women are executive assistants, professional project managers, communication directors, and savvy logistics specialists—without whom corporations would have difficulty conducting their day-to-day business. In many cases, gatekeepers have a clearer perspective than their supervisor about internal politics, converging timelines, and budgetary issues. It's vital that you rethink how you perceive and engage gatekeepers.

> *"Gatekeepers are no longer "stepping stones" to the executive level. Many are executive assistants, managers, communication directors, and savvy logistics specialists."*

Let's begin by agreeing on five observations we should keep in mind as we map a pathway to the executive buyer.

- There is no single action or "silver bullet" that guarantees you will get in front of an executive buyer.
- There are steps you can take to improve your probability of securing an appointment, and there are actions you should set aside because they could weaken your chances for success. You must be flexible.
- Success in getting time with your executive target has far less to do with scripts, clever lines, and "sound bites" than with cultivating a sustainable relationship with a gatekeeper.
- Senior executives are not the only people who employ gatekeepers. In many organizations, there are administrative tiers that protect and insulate mid-level managers and department heads.
- You need to broaden your concept of gatekeepers, their role, and capabilities.

The Harsh Realities of Getting Past Gatekeepers

An important step in rethinking the role of the gatekeeper is to understand the harsh realities that surround a seller's plan to gain access to an executive buyer.

1. It's harder than ever to gain a spot on an executive's calendar. Why? You are competing with high-priority initiatives that have immediate time frames.

2. You may encounter more than one gatekeeper. Why? Project managers can be found at different levels and function in roles like an administrative assistant, technical specialist, or assistant to the vice president.

3. You have a better chance of getting past a gatekeeper if you are an incumbent supplier. Why? Gatekeepers may assume that meetings will cover ongoing services. You and your company may be a trusted partner or provider.

4. You have a better chance of getting on an executive's calendar early in the buying process. Why? That is when executives are curious about what is going on in their industry, what solutions are available, and what problems others may have experienced.

5. Executive buyers seldom listen to your voice messages. Why? Administrative aides are often charged with reviewing executives' voice mails and providing "triage." In short, they decide which messages will go forward and which ones will die a quick, silent death.

6. Access is often defined by an internal set of protocols. Why? RFP processes may outline who can be accessed and when access stops. Also, many buying organizations develop internal guidelines to insure compliance with industry or government regulations when choosing suppliers.

UNLOCKING THE MIND OF THE GATEKEEPER

Let's review the roles and power of gatekeepers and then look at how you can best tap into how they view their evolving roles and responsibilities.

The Role of the Gatekeeper

Gatekeeper roles take on a combination of four primary responsibilities:

- Keeping the wrong people out
- Allowing the right people in
- Making sure the right people are referred to the right executive
- Protecting and respecting an executive's priorities

Think of gatekeepers as "talent scouts" and "vice presidents of access."

Questions to Consider When Qualifying a Gatekeeper

As you begin the process of identifying a potential blocker, gatekeeper, and process manager, ask yourself five questions so you can better understand the role and influence of a gatekeeper.

- Does this individual have the power to help me access influential stakeholders and buyers?
- If I proceed in the wrong direction, does this individual have the knowledge to help me correct my plan?
- Does this individual have knowledge of informal alliances that might influence how buyers decide?
- Does this individual have knowledge of the buying process and time frames?
- In addition to being a gatekeeper, does this individual play an influential role in the buying process?

How Does a Gatekeeper Think?

Several blogs, posts, and articles have reported comments from gatekeepers of different roles and ranks in their organizations. We have compiled comments from our experience and research on how they conduct their screening responsibilities. They are very informative, and we share a sample of their comments here.

- *"I turn away or turn down between 10 and 20 calls a day from sellers."*
- *"I can't be bullied. Trying to push your way in just won't work."*
- *"I tell most callers 'He's not in.' That line usually stops them cold."*
- *"I need to know the 'why' behind any meeting or phone call. You've got to give me something worthwhile for my boss."*
- *"Most sales people don't know enough about how we operate to know who they should be seeing. I spend a fair amount of time redirecting and referring."*

One staff manager who controls access to a senior vice president of operations explained that most sales people assume she graduated from a secretarial school. *"They would be amazed to learn that I have an MBA, that I make more than any of our department heads, and that I've served four senior vice presidents over the last twelve years."* She isn't just a gatekeeper: she is an office manager, team leader, operations executive, communication director, talent scout, and vice president of access.

Every gatekeeper wants to know two things when you call: what value do you bring, and what's the urgency?

Who Is the Gatekeeper?

Gatekeepers' titles and functions vary with different selling opportunities. Here are some gatekeeper titles.

- Administrative assistant
- Executive assistant
- Receptionist
- Assistant vice president
- Project manager
- Procurement agent
- Assistant to the vice president
- Chief of staff
- Office manager

Administrative Assistant vs. Executive Assistant

So, what's the difference between an "admin" and an executive assistant? It's a big one. An administrative assistant may have access to the executive's calendar but no power to add or change appointments. They have little or no knowledge of business priorities, so they cannot judge what's urgent and critical. Most "admins" are hourly staff who move from office to office depending on staffing needs. But this doesn't mean they can't provide valuable information. Consider some questions that you may wish to explore with an administrative assistant.

- Is she (executive buyer) in today?
- Do you expect her in later today?
- Are you her administrative aid?
- What is her formal title?
- What is her email address?

You may be thinking, "This isn't going to get me an appointment with the executive buyer." Maybe not, but it can provide you with some valuable information that may help along the way.

On the other hand, executive assistants are usually salaried employees with relatively longer tenure in their position. In fact, many have been in their position longer than the executive buyer. Here are some questions for an executive assistant. They could yield vital bits of information for you, the seller.

- Can you get me 15 minutes of their time for a phone call later this week?
- Is she attending the national meeting (convention, conference, or trade show) in Chicago in two weeks?
- Who are some of the internal stakeholders involved in the decision?
- How does this project rank as a priority?

- Sometimes projects like this end up falling into the lap of the smartest person in the room—the executive assistant. What role are you playing in the process?
- How could I get access to a current organizational chart?

The executive assistant is likely to know more about budgets, timelines, meetings, participants, corporate politics, and availability. The key point here is to gain more information every time you get someone on the phone—whether they are an administrative assistant or an executive assistant. Always remember, they can say to their CEO or executive, "I think you should talk (or not) to this person."

WHAT ARE THE THREE TYPES OF GATEKEEPERS?

It's worth noting that gatekeepers come in different shapes and sizes. The three most common types of gatekeepers are shown in Figure 5–1:

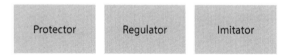

Figure 5-1 Three Types of Gatekeepers

- **The Protector** is a "blocker" who stands between the seller and the executive buyer. Protectors may be an administrative assistant, receptionist, or office manager. They work side by side with an executive and insulate the executive from unwanted or unsolicited intrusions—emails, meetings, appointments, and phone calls. Most protectors know the "soft spots" in an executive's calendar—those events that can be easily rescheduled or cancelled.

  Recommended Action: Often the Protector is the target of "push and shove" artists that attempt to bully their way in. Protectors often feel unappreciated by outsiders. If you want to win over a Protector, consider the following tactics:

1. **Present the gatekeeper with a problem, and ask their advice.** For example, you might say, "I'm unfamiliar with the reporting lines. With whom should I speak about meeting your new supplier criteria?"

2. **Craft a powerful reason for the meeting.** For example, you may have "follow-up" information from a previous call or appointment. You may have time-sensitive material on pricing or recent product-testing results. Be specific about what you need and the value you provide.

3. **Use a referral from someone internal or well-known to the executive.** With some Protectors, referrals may be the best or only way to get to the executive buyer. If you can cite a trusted colleague or team player, this could go a long way toward getting on the calendar.

   For example, "Bill Foster, CEO of _____, suggested that I contact _____ because we just helped Bill's team improve operational efficiency by 15% with our technology, and he thought we might be able to produce similar results for your firm. Could you help me set up a 15-minute call to see if there is a synergism between your needs and our capabilities?"

- **The Regulator** controls part or all of the buying and decision-making process. Their formal title may be Committee Chair, Purchasing Agent or Project Manager. They feel responsible for creating a "level playing field" with "rules that are meant to be followed." These folks regulate when it's appropriate to apply requirements and when it's okay to look away.

  Recommended Action: Regulators are frequently the target of tricks, deceptions, and ploys. Sellers often take great measures to avoid the Regulator and go straight to their target. Regulators set rules to protect themselves and the processes they are charged with governing. Tip: You might consider either of the following approaches:

1. **If a requirement or regulation is unreasonable, show the Regulator a solid reason for changing or overlooking the rules.** Explain the implications for the buying process. For example, you might explain that if you can't collect and verify firsthand what the buyer needs, you won't be able to submit a timely proposal. If the size, scope, or cost of a product or service warrants an executive level discussion, Regulators may find it difficult to turn down or dismiss your request for an executive-level meeting. There is no guarantee for success, but this scenario may prompt the Regulator to forward your meeting request irrespective of rules and protocols.

2. **Ask for a "top2top" appointment.** At times, Regulators find it difficult to turn down or dismiss requests for executive-level meetings. While there is no guarantee of success, the Regulator may find it necessary to forward the request irrespective of rules and protocols. The size, scope, or cost of a product or service may warrant an executive-level discussion.

- **The Imitator** creates the pretense of being the executive buyer. This individual thrives on being in the spotlight. They claim to be the final authority when, in truth, the Imitator works closely with a senior-level executive, the real decision-maker. Sometimes it's hard to distinguish between the Imitator and the actual executive buyer and to know who really has the power to move an initiative forward when it includes the purchase of your product or service.

  Recommended Action: While this individual may not have final authority, they are still highly engaged and influential in the buying process. These tactics may be useful as you confirm who is who.

  1. **Treat them as the boss.** Ask for the Imitator's help and assume they are the decision-maker. Most Imitators want to be helpful—especially to their boss. Be specific about what you need and the value you provide. Imitators know what is important

to their boss and when to defer to the executive in charge. Treat them properly and turn them into an advocate. Make your telephone call a personal conversation between you and them. Remember, sales representatives are calling them constantly trying to get an appointment with their boss. Leverage their knowledge, and stand out as a professional.

For example, "Mary I wonder if you could help me? When I listened to _____'s recent telephone call with the analysts following your firm, I heard him say that one of his areas of focus in the next year was going to be improving your firm's IT capability. My organization has extensive experience helping firms your size in your industry. We've helped them increase their capabilities on time and under budget. Could I send you some information and then set up a time to review it with you? After our call, you could decide to give it to _____ or help me set up a meeting. Is that acceptable to you?"

This approach allows you to obtain their email address, so you can communicate at any time. It will also provide the format for the executive's email address.

2. **Go around them.** This approach is dangerous because it can create an enemy that makes life miserable for you even if you do get the appointment and/or the sale. This tactic should be used with extreme caution and only when time is running out and you have no other course of action and no revenue within the account.

THE CARE & FEEDING OF A GATEKEEPER

Gatekeepers are not "throwaways" you can discard once you feel confident you'll win the opportunity. Why? Most gatekeepers survive changes in leadership ranks, mergers, downsizing, and reorganizations. Your prospects and buyers seem to come and go, while gatekeepers can be near-permanent fixtures. While building a relationship with a gatekeeper, capitalize on your opportunities, and consider avoiding some of the following mistakes.

Four Fatal Mistakes When Working with Gatekeepers

1. Don't lie to a gatekeeper. If you misrepresent your intentions, you can make the gatekeeper appear like he/she hasn't performed their job competently. This could come back to haunt you[1].

2. Don't try to "game" them. Forget trying to call the boss before or after hours. They are experienced and have seen and dealt with every trick designed to get past them. Your chances of getting through are minimal with caller ID. Even if the boss answers, he won't know you or appreciate receiving your unsolicited call.

3. Don't manipulate. Give them respect and acknowledgement, but don't try an overt sell. Be personable, and draw them out of their business role. Show them how they can win with your help.

4. Don't get pushy. Most gatekeepers are well versed in handling bullies. All the red flags pop up when they feel threatened or trapped.

How Can the Gatekeeper Assist the Seller?

In any meeting or conversation with a gatekeeper, you should have a very simple three-part objective in mind[2].

1. Discover the gatekeeper's range of knowledge of the organization, the decision process, and the role of any stakeholders.

2. Discover the gatekeeper's range of responsibility. Are they limited to an administrative role? Do they have project-management responsibility? Do they have procedural oversight on how decisions are made?

3. Determine to what extent the gatekeeper is willing to accommodate your interests. Are they willing to make referrals and provide information?

With any approach, you must carefully plan your engagement with a gatekeeper. Remember the adage: "Proper planning prevents poor performance." Plan at the tactical level:

- Change your mindset. Instead of thinking of them as gatekeepers, think of them as talent scouts or vice presidents of access who conduct the initial interview on behalf of the buying organization.
- Get their name, and write it down. You may need to talk to them several times, so document their contact information.
- Treat them with respect. Most people don't. Remember, a gatekeeper spends more hours per day with their boss than they do with their spouse. Treat them as professionals. They are only trying to do their job.
- Craft a business benefit they will receive as a result of your meeting. Be clear, concise, honest, and polite about why you are calling. They know their company better than you and may direct you to someone else. Respect their guidance.

TOOLS (OLD & NEW) FOR ACCESSING THE EXECUTIVE

Gatekeeper strategies are just one set of "tools" available to help the savvy seller penetrate the executive ranks of an organization. Your access strategy requires more than the cultivation of a sustainable relationship with a gatekeeper.

Is "Cold Calling" Really Dead?

No, of course not. However, in many industries it is a low-probability tactic that forces you through barriers and over more speed bumps and potholes than is worth the effort. Security provisions in many companies make in-person cold calls impossible. Regarding phone calls, focus more on the gatekeeper than the executive buyer. Don't try to shove the door open. Develop a relationship that encourages the gatekeeper to open the door for you.

Where's the Blind Spot?

Most executive buyers, senior managers, and C-suite executives have an obvious "blind spot" that many top producers leverage to connect with their targets. Conferences, conventions, and exhibitions are the executive's "blind spot." Why? For most executives, a conference or convention is an opportunity to escape the pressure of daily issues, reports, phone calls, and inter-office politics that complicate their work environment.

Conferences provide unstructured time that can be allocated as the executive wishes. They can have coffee with a colleague or listen to the keynote address. They can attend a panel discussion on issues in their field or visit booths in the exhibition hall. The point is, there is no gatekeeper, blocker, or calendar marshal controlling one's activities.

> **Recommended Action:** Top performers often develop a plan well in advance of the conference to maximize their opportunity to connect with a handful of key executive-level targets. These are some of the tips they have shared:
>
> - Identify and prioritize a list of 5 or 6 "must meet" targets.
> - Research each target's likely activities, and plan a point of contact.
> - Who is presenting or participating in a panel discussion? This is a great opportunity to attend their session and meet them after their presentation.
> - Are targets likely to attend an opening reception? By definition, receptions are alcohol-laced and unstructured. It's a great opportunity to approach a potential buyer.
> - Who knows your target? Perhaps a mutual acquaintance could arrange to invite the target to lunch, dinner, or coffee.
> - Keep the group of colleagues on "booth duty" apprised of your list of "must meet" targets. Make sure they call or text you if one visits the booth.
> - Plan dinners and invite targets as well as current customers.
> - Conferences are great places to connect, however, executives don't like to be bombarded by sales people trying to sell them. The best tactic may be to secure a commitment for a follow-up conversation after the conference.
> - Secure an opportunity to speak at a conference. It builds credibility, even if you are the moderator.

Too often sellers spend their time complaining about booth duty, hoping some executive buyer will miraculously stumble over to the booth and express interest in their product. That's always possible, but not probable.

Can Social Media Help?

Absolutely! The capabilities of social media are as broad as your imagination. Social media is expanding and changing in ways that were unthinkable several years ago. But you'll need to establish a foundation. And you'll need to know what you're looking for and what you want to achieve. Let's look at a short list of capabilities that may improve a seller's ability to get past the gatekeeper and connect with an executive buyer.

Challenge: "I need a referral that my executive will respect." A seller might want to do some research on LinkedIn to identify network members in common. Track your buyer on LinkedIn or Twitter.

Challenge: "I need to uncover the challenges and issues facing my executive." Follow the target company on LinkedIn or Inside View, and create a listening post with Twitter.

Challenge: "I need to determine what percentage of buyers are considering an alternative form of financing when they purchase." Poll your connections on LinkedIn.

Challenge: "My target is delivering a keynote address at a conference that I will be attending. How can I show my support?" Send your comments or questions via Twitter.

We all want to get to the boss or the relevant executive that will make the final decision. This connection is natural, important, and often required to win the sale. However, we must remember that if we are successful in getting to the boss or relevant executive, and if we get the sale, it could be very valuable to have the gatekeeper on our side. They can help us navigate unknowns and other landmines that may surface. We should strive to make them our ally.

Key Points to Remember

1. It's harder than ever to get an appointment on an executive buyer's calendar.

2. In a complex B2B sale, you may find yourself encountering more than one gatekeeper.

3. The responsibility of a gatekeeper is four-fold: keep the wrong people out, let the right people in, refer the right people to the right people, and protect and respect an executive buyer's priorities.

4. A gatekeeper can be an administrative assistant, a project manager, an assistant vice president, or department head—to name a few titles.

5. Administrative assistants and executive assistants have different roles, knowledge, and power.

6. There are three types of gatekeeper: Protectors, Regulators, and Imitators.

7. There are several tactics that you should avoid at all costs. Don't get pushy. Don't be deceptive. Don't manipulate. They can make you lose. Remember—if you win, you'll have to work with the gatekeeper.

8. Gatekeepers often have vital information that you need: What is the buyer's commitment to the status quo? How do buyers view your product and company? What timeline are they working on? When's their next meeting?

9. Remember that a national meeting, conference, or trade show is a "blind spot" in your prospect's schedule. Have a plan to connect with your list of prospects.

10. Change your mindset. Don't think of them as gatekeepers. They assess your value and benefit to the buying organization.

11. Cold calling isn't dead, but you'll need to develop a positive relationship with the gatekeeper to breach all the obstacles facing you.

12. Social media can help in several ways: get a referral, track your buyer, and understand what's important to your buyer.

——— YOUR COMMITMENT ———

What is the one thing you will commit to doing differently because of reading this chapter? Please share it here or on a separate sheet of paper.

_____

_____

_____

_____

Chapter 6

Better Eat Your Wheaties

Selling Against the Status Quo

"The status quo bias, your prospect's natural resistance to doing something different, is the biggest threat to your success—bigger, I would argue, than the other competitors in your industry."

Tim Riesterer—Author of *Conversations that Win the Complex Sale*

Don't underestimate the power of internal solutions or incumbent suppliers. The status quo can be a strongly entrenched, competitive force with executive supporters. It can have an impressive performance record with documented costs, risks, and benefits. Be careful, and be prepared!

The Story: Who's the Competition?

Several years ago, we were training a group of sales managers for a life sciences company in North Carolina. During lunch, one of the managers raised a question: "I've always wondered why one of our competitors seems to dominate the Southwest market while we hold the dominant position in the Midwest. Is this just history, or is there something I'm missing?" Managers offered explanations that ranged from proximity to corporate headquarters to the location of top sales producers. It was a lively, engaging discussion until one manager threw a curve ball: "I don't mind other suppliers. I can't begrudge them winning their share of the business because we'll always win ours. That's the nature of business. What I hate is going through a lengthy sales process, spending hours driving from Chicago to Detroit, taking people I don't know to lunch or dinner only to find that the customer decided to stay with their current supplier. In fact, the status quo might just be the market leader in the upper Midwest."

Our friend from St. Charles, IL, was correct. In fact, many markets are dominated by this shadowy, elusive, and powerful competitor called "the status quo." Too many sellers take the status quo as a fragile, arcane solution that can be pushed aside easily. Well . . . better eat your Wheaties! You're going to need strength to compete with the status quo.

> **Seller's Challenge:** *Build a Strategy to Compete Effectively Against the Status Quo*
>
> Sellers must understand an incumbent's value to the buying organization, capture how to communicate the real costs of doing nothing, and counteract sources of support and sponsorship for the status quo. Sellers may face political issues and alliances that put them at a disadvantage when competing for the deal.

As you'll discover in this chapter, sellers must learn how to combine logical and emotional appeals, so they can change a buyer's perspective of the status quo and maximize their opportunity to win.

WHAT IS THE STATUS QUO?

What do we mean by the "status quo?" The answer is a bit more complex than the question. In Latin, the phrase *status quo*, means "current conditions" or the "current state of affairs." We have come to use "status quo" as a generic reference to a broad range of conditions, situations, events, and requirements "as they exist." If a friend asks you about your situation at home, she would be referring to something unsaid. It could refer to your difficulty in getting the family to agree on a vacation or to relationship issues with your teenaged son. If you were to answer "status quo," it would mean things are "unchanged," "the same," or "no better or worse."

When a seller speaks of the status quo, his/her point of reference is the conditions, events, and business processes impacted by some existing product, service, or solution. The seller may be referring to an incumbent supplier, an internal solution, or the absence of any solution at all. On the other hand, the buyer may have a much "richer" perspective of the status quo. Through the lens of a buyer, the status quo may include the feelings and emotions associated with the creation and implementation of the product or solution.

Let's consider a simple example. A CFO for a medium-sized college is interested in replacing the college's antiquated financial-services software. While there are many systems on the market, the prices seem out of range. The CIO assures the CFO that his team is willing to modify the existing system, but the CFO realizes there are drawbacks. It will take six months; they will need a modest hardware budget, and they will need to bring on some contract programmers who have experience in financial services.

When the CFO thinks about the status quo, he envisions all the capabilities, limitations, benefits, and costs associated with the modified system (cognitive elements). His thoughts also embrace the emotional elements: the frustrations, concerns, sleepless nights, arguments, and pride associated with the process. For buyers like this CFO, the status quo combines cognitive and emotional elements. Many sellers never see this broader perspective because they are looking for a limited range of cognitive elements—product performance, reliability, and cost.

Status quo as a competitive force can embrace any of the following decisions:

- **Buyer chooses to do nothing**, either because a new purchase holds low priority or the cost of doing nothing is not understood.

- **Buyer chooses to retain an internally generated product or solution:** no change in the status of their current solutions.
- **Buyer chooses to retain an incumbent supplier**: no change in current vendor agreements and contracts.
- **Buyer chooses to retain a hybrid or patchwork solution** that includes some combination of suppliers, third parties, and/or internal resources.

Buyers who like the status quo are NOT receptive to change. This factor must be taken into consideration when selling *against* the status quo. Some stakeholders are fine with their current system even without all the techno-rich "bells and whistles." Other buyers are tired of the headaches and want a new solution right away.

WHAT ARE THE MYTHS & REALITIES FACING UNWARY SELLERS?

Let's consider how we, the sellers, can better grasp the complexity of competing against the status quo.

 "Most sellers miscalculate and misjudge the benefits and internal support for the status quo."

Eight Harsh Realities for the Unwary Seller

1. **The status quo is a market leader**. 23.8 % of all opportunities sellers forecast they will win are not awarded.[1] This means that most sellers miscalculate and misjudge the benefits and internal support for the status quo. (Think about the additional revenue and profit you would capture if you could win just a small fraction of these deals!)
2. **Ties go to the incumbent**. Unless the current solution is broken, retaining the status quo is easier, safer, and less costly for the buyer. Our friends in social psychology refer to an individual's "preference for stability" over change. There are two factors to consider. First,

people tend to respond in ways that justify prior decisions. The stakeholder purchased the product for a reason, and often they are comfortable with the brand, company, and personnel. If a change is made, the buyer may be concerned it will give the impression that he/she made the wrong initial choice. Second, the stakeholder may not perceive any major difference between two solutions and may not want to take the time required to change. In addition, the cost of change may be high and disruptive, so even small advantages on your side may not override their resistance to change.

3. **Internal solutions may appear to be less expensive, even with evidence to the contrary.** In other words, the "cost of inaction" is perceived to be low. Why? Often "hidden costs" and "soft costs" are not considered when comparing an existing solution to a new one. Sellers can create great value by showing the true costs of inaction early in the sales process.

4. **Information overload makes differentiation difficult.** Busy stakeholders are forced to process new information and make a complicated decision. They find it difficult to distinguish your solution from their existing solution.

5. **Fear of blame or repercussions can result in no change**. The status quo often appears to be the lowest risk and least painful solution. No one wants to lose his/her job or be blamed for a new solution that didn't work as expected. Stakeholders may be concerned with the time required for training, testing, or implementing. If buyers are risk averse, outside vendors may fight a losing battle.

6. **Internal sponsors or mobilizers can lead informal campaigns that discredit external competitors**. An outside supplier may lose without ever knowing why or how. Internal forces may stack the cards against a solution that is unproven, costly, or time-consuming.

7. **Incumbent suppliers know the system.** Incumbents are far better than sellers at understanding organizational politics and using informal communication channels to advance their cause and undermine their competition.

8. **Users have a loud voice**. Those stakeholders in charge of using or managing the product or solution have a disproportionate voice when deciding to retain a supplier or do nothing.

Six Myths About Selling Against the Status Quo

The relationship between the status quo and the stakeholders is often unclear to someone on the outside. Sellers often take a stakeholder's perspective of the status quo at face value—which reveals only part of the story. Consider the following six myths that confound many sellers.

1. **When a buying organization solicits a bid or proposal, it shows they are dissatisfied with their current supplier or solution.** Absolutely not! The buying organization may want a free consult and a price quote that will give them leverage when negotiating with a current supplier.
2. **Impressive and lengthy client lists give external suppliers an edge**. Nope. Buyers are less interested in length and more interested in a small group of comparable accounts within their industry. They want an apples-to-apples comparison.
3. **Choosing to "do nothing" is just a waiting game—eventually buyers will "see the light" and decide to buy.** Again, no. Buyers may decide that outside solutions are too expensive, complicated, or risky. The decision to "do nothing" may be a signal that the project is a low priority and not worth the pain.
4. **A "no" means "no."** It may also mean "not now." Higher-priority initiatives may push lower-priority initiatives into the future. This may change the time frame of the sale, but it doesn't necessarily eliminate the opportunity.
5. **Most internal solutions are Band-Aid fixes that won't last.** Don't be deceived—many internal solutions are quite sophisticated, highly customized, and cost-effective.
6. **Buyers want the latest-and-greatest product release or software version.** Not true. Many buyers believe that "good is good enough."

A product upgrade (by itself) is insufficient grounds for switching suppliers. Far too many buyers have been burned by new products that claimed to provide more value but failed to live up to the seller's promise.

HOW TO DEVELOP A SALES STRATEGY TO ATTACK THE STATUS QUO

While the status quo is our most common and successful competitor, you can't just ignore every account with an entrenched supplier or homegrown solution. However, you can do your homework, research your prospect, and assess how committed the stakeholders are to the status quo. This means understanding a buyer's "perspective" on the status quo—his or her unique algorithm of business (cognitive) and personal (emotional) reflections.

Let's see how six core elements can help you research, prepare, and execute a strategy to compete with the status quo:

- Read the Signs
- Conduct a Discovery Process
- Ask, "Why Buy Now?"
- Embrace the Emotional Sell
- Create Differentiation
- Break the Rules

Read the Signs

In every sale, there are cues that help sellers assess the buying context. How receptive are the stakeholders to change? How entrenched is the supplier? What role does politics play? Consider signs that show the status quo is untouchable and indicators that the status quo may be vulnerable to an effective sales strategy.

Signs the Status Quo May Be Firmly Entrenched. As you assess your competitive position, you may want to consider the following signs that indicate the buying organization is unlikely to change. It's important to have situational awareness and best to read the warning signs before committing time and resources to an unwinnable opportunity. Here are signs that may forewarn you of difficulties in winning the deal.

1. **"Dynamic Value Messaging"[2] Doesn't Resonate with Buyers**
   - Your value message is out of sync with the buyer's journey. It's the wrong message at the wrong time.
   - Your return on investment is unclear, undocumented, or irrelevant.
   - Your value message doesn't differentiate your product or solution.
   - Stakeholders are challenging the efficacy of your claim.

2. **Stakeholders See Too Much Risk in Change**
   - A history of unplanned supply shortfalls and performance problems can heighten stakeholders' fears of change.
   - Internal users portray change as having significant risk when they are really supporting their own comfort level with the status quo.

3. **The Incumbent Supplier Is Entrenched**
   - The incumbent supplier is copied on all buyer correspondence.
   - The incumbent supplier participates in planning processes with the buying organization.
   - The incumbent supplier scores high marks on the "supplier score card."
   - The incumbent supplier has been diligent in measuring and addressing product-performance issues.
   - The incumbent supplier's pricing is appropriate to the market and account size.
   - The incumbent supplier has one or more internal Champions. In turn, the seller is having difficulty garnering support from stakeholders.

4. **Poor Timing for a Buying Process**
   - If a buyer has recently implemented another solution that's similar to yours, they probably don't need another solution right now. It's a timing issue.
   - Sometimes buyers don't have the time, effort, or inclination to conduct due diligence on a new product.

5. **Difficulty of Buyer in Differentiating Among Competing Solutions**
   - There are two underlying issues: discomfort in deciding, and not knowing how to distinguish among options.
   - Some sellers effectively present claims that make their product appear to be the market leader.

6. **Buyer Preference for Stability**
   - The buyer purchased the product for a reason, and often they are comfortable with the product, brand, company, and personnel. Making a change could be viewed by others as a fix for their wrong initial choice. Their tendency is to respond in ways that justify their earlier decision.
   - The buyer may not perceive any major difference between two products.

7. **The Intrusion of Competing Projects and Initiatives**
   - Resources are tight in every organization. Sometimes other projects have the priority over a competing project.
   - The firm is in the process of a merger, acquisition, or divestiture.
   - The seller finds it difficult to engage stakeholders.

8. **The Presence of a Strong Internal Solution**
   - The internal solution was commissioned by the CEO or other member of the executive team.
   - The internal solution was formulated to address a unique set of circumstances that your product may not fully satisfy.
   - The buying organization's internal solution was supported by external consultants (e.g. KPMG or Accenture) who are well connected to the executive team.
   - The internal solution was a joint venture with one of your strongest competitors; while the solution appears to be internally generated, parts of the solutions are supported by a reputable supplier.
   - The internal solution has a documented history of success and strong ROI.

- It doesn't require start-up costs and marketing expenses, which makes it inexpensive by comparison.

Signs the Status Quo May Be Receptive to Change. While the status quo can be a formidable opponent, there are many instances where there are clear signs of receptivity to change. Here are some signs that the status quo may be vulnerable.

1. Stakeholders and users openly talk about a trigger event that concerns them. Think: problem, opportunity or threat.
2. Stakeholders are convinced that funding is available for a costlier solution.
3. Executives are open and available for discussion.
4. Sellers perceive an air of openness and accessibility.
5. Executives support a discovery process that focuses on the size, scope, and urgency of the situation.
6. Lower-level users are interested in discussing implementation, training, and time frames.
7. There is an internal sponsor or mobilizer championing change.
8. Stakeholders are interested in talking to colleagues at other companies about their solution.
9. The current supplier is taking the account for granted.
10. New leadership is fostering a culture of change.

While warning signs are just indicators, they will give you a pretty good initial read on obstacles to change or internal concerns that either support or impede your sales strategy.

Conduct a Discovery Process

Top-performing sellers often use a discovery process to probe and understand the customer's issues, concerns, problems, opportunities, and threats.

Anthony Iannarino writes, "Discovery is about learning what your client needs, their strategic indicatives, their goals, and their outcomes.

Discovery work is what allows you to neatly tie anything you propose to what your client needs and to tailor it to those specific needs."[3]

Consultants often plan a discovery stage early in a project. When designing a plan for attacking the status quo, structure your discovery efforts around the issues. Consider these questions around which your discovery efforts could be structured.

- Are stakeholders receptive to change?
- What are the sources of power and support for the status quo?
- Who is aligned with whom (politically)?
- What obstacles have prevented change in the past?
- What's the size, scope, and urgency of the problem?
- Has there been a trigger event that is "front of mind" for stakeholders?
- Is the opportunity winnable?
- If winnable, is the opportunity good business?

In an ideal world, you could ask these questions directly and get accurate answers. In truth, discovery is a probing process that requires elements of subtlety, hypothesis testing, misdirection, and provocation. While it may be inappropriate to ask some questions directly, consider the following 24 questions you may be able to ask the buyer. Whether you can ask them directly or not, answers to questions like these can help you differentiate the problem from a symptom of the problem.

1. What problems are "top of mind"?
2. What difficulties or challenges has this problem caused? On a 1-10 scale, how important is it to resolve this problem?
3. What individuals and departments have been hurt most by this problem? What has been the impact?
4. How have you (the organization) attempted to solve the problem? What challenges have you encountered?
5. What resources (expertise, personnel, capital, time) have you relied on to solve the problem?

6. If unresolved, how will this problem impact corporate goals?
7. How satisfied are you with your current supplier?
8. What two or three actions should your supplier have taken to resolve this problem?
9. In your opinion, what's the cause of your problem?
10. Why is it a high priority today?
11. What would an effective solution look like?
12. What are your obstacles to implementing a solution?
13. What's your timeline for achieving a solution?
14. Is adequate funding in place to solve the problem?
15. Who is responsible for the funding?
16. Who else will play a role in choosing a supplier?
17. Do you have formal criteria for selecting a supplier? Who compiled these criteria?
18. What's the process for purchasing the product?
19. Which stakeholders are likely to influence the decision?
20. Which stakeholders are interested in exploring a possible change? Which are not?
21. What reasons do you hear for not changing?
22. Are there political issues surrounding the decision to change?
23. How informed are stakeholders about their options in the market today?
24. Are there other, more pressing, issues the organization must solve before this one?

It's important to remember that discovery is an ongoing process and not a question-and-answer event.

Why Buy Now?

The status quo is a dangerous, competitive force. Buyers can be lulled easily into over-confidence and fail to see urgency or a threat driving the need to change. "We don't need to rush into a decision. Things seem to be going well." If the seller fails to craft a compelling case for immediate change, then they may see the buying process slow down, falter, and then stop. Instead of a temporary halt, the buying process flounders and dies. It wasn't that the seller didn't get to the right buyers or offer a competitive price—it was a failure to create a message that communicated a sense of urgency, an impending threat, or the risk of retaining the status quo.

Understand the situation from the buyer's perspective. While the seller may offer an attractive package of benefits with the purchase of their product or solution, there are lingering concerns, fears, and suspicions. Top performers understand that they must assuage these unvoiced threats. But they understand a more important challenge: "How can I transfer the perceived risk from my product to the status quo?" For the buyer, it's not just a matter of "What will I gain from a new product?" It's a question of "What will I lose, jeopardize, or put at risk by my reluctance to change now?"

The team of researchers at Corporate Visions reports that "Executives are 70 percent more willing to make a risky business decision, like changing from their current situation to an alternative, if you frame their status quo in terms of what they stand to lose versus what they stand to gain."[4] They refer to this as "Why Now" messaging.

As you build your strategy, give thought to sources of risk in retaining the status quo that have gone unrecognized and may pose threats in the near term, such as obsolete parts or materials, the inability to support new revenue streams, and the drain on internal resources necessary to sustain the product.

Embrace the "Emotional Sell"

How often have sales managers told you "Customers buy for emotional reasons and justify on rational grounds."? Enough said. Now we're going to prove it and show you what you can do about it while planning your sales strategy for competing with the status quo.

What Does Neuroscience Tells Us About the Status Quo? Decisions are a combination of logic and emotion. Understanding how logic and emotion speak into our decisions can help us develop content that influences buying decisions. Recent research in neuroscience and neuro-marketing provides valuable insight.

Let's start with the key points that tie logic and emotion into the buying process. Two parts of the brain are involved. The cerebral cortex, often termed the "New Brain," drives logic. The cerebellum (mid-brain) controls emotion.

The logic portion of our brain demands evidence and proof of results. It wants cold, hard facts. Proof, test results, and performance measures can be highly effective in stimulating the logic portion of our brain. This "new brain" responds well to Return on Investment (ROI), Net Present Value (NPV), Internal Rate of Return (IRR), Payback, Total Cost of Ownership (TCO), and Cost of Inaction (COI).

The emotional portion of our brain addresses safety and survival. It detests risk. In fact, the emotional part of our brain is two times more likely to avoid risk than pursue gain. It quickly determines if a change is warranted. Its natural tendency is to avoid change and retain the status quo.

Figure 6–1 compares emotion and logic. Emotion is personal, intuitive, and responds quickly. Logic responds slowly, is rational, and requires reasoning and proof. Give thought to how you complement the reasoning process by stimulating the buyer's emotions.

Emotion	Logic
Pride, Image, Surprise, Fear of Loss, Concern	Key Performance Indicators: % to Goal
Annoyance, Irritation, Anger, Gratification, Embarrassment	Business Results: Cost Savings, Speed
Touch, Control, Confidence	Financial Metrics: ROI, NPV, IRR, Payback, TCO, COI
Ease of Use, Gratitude	Operational Metrics: Time to Performance

Figure 6-1 Emotion Versus Logic

A 2015 CEB (now CEB-Gartner) study looked at how emotion influenced B2B buying and found the following differences between business value (cognitive) and personal value (emotional) as shown in Figure 6–2.[5]

Business Value	Personal Value
48% of B2B customers say they have wanted to buy a new solution but haven't spoken up for fear of risk	Personal value has 2X as much impact as business value
74% of B2B buyers see a business value	68% of buyers who see a personal value will pay a higher price for a service
Just 14% of B2B buyers perceive a real difference in B2B supplier offerings	Only 8.5% of buyers who don't see personal value will pay a higher price for a product
Only 31% of prospective customers think B2B brands provide a personal value	71% of buyers who see a personal value will purchase a product

Figure 6-2 Business Value Versus Personal Value

The data is very compelling, isn't it? It seems clear that, if sellers can communicate both a business and personal value, they will substantially increase their probability of winning the sales opportunity.

If the data isn't convincing, the study also found that 71% of buyers who see personal value purchase a B2B product versus 22.6% who don't purchase without seeing a personal value. A greater proportion of B2B customers are emotionally attached to the brand they purchased than are B2C customers. The reason is simple. A B2B purchase entails much more personal risk.

If an individual chooses to purchase the wrong size television or the wrong color car, they simply live with it. If they make the wrong decision about a large company purchase, they risk losing a bonus or a job or a promotion. The negative impact can reach all aspects of one's professional and personal life.

As you contemplate integrating logic and emotion, think of emotion as having a number of levers that you can press. Have you convinced the stakeholder that your solution is safe? Has your product been tested elsewhere successfully? Is there a precise road map for implementation? Are other members of the buying group supportive of your time lines? What is your guarantee that the product will work? Have you pressed all the levers so that the stakeholder will see your solution as "can't fail."

So, what are the teaching points from the research on the "emotional sell" that can be applied to selling against the status quo?

When a seller conveys a message that combines business (cognitive) and personal (emotional) value, here is what they can expect:

- Buyers are far more likely to buy
- Buyers are far more likely to buy at a higher price

Why Do Emotions Rule Buying Decisions? The reason is simple. As humans, we are trained to recognize objective or cognitive value. It is easy to know the superiority of one number over another. Cognitive value is easily supported by logic, documentation, and measurement. While cognitive value is certainly required to meet the logical needs of the cerebral cortex, it doesn't meet the demands of the "mid-brain" that controls emotion.

Strong emotional connections can drive a buyer in one direction or another despite graphs, charts, and KPIs. How do we create these emotional connections? There are five ways:

- A buyer can **experience** a trigger event that gives rise to feelings like fear, anger, confusion and desperation along with product failures, unexpected downtime, repair costs, etc.
- A buyer can **witness** circumstances that happen to someone like him or her—perhaps a neighbor, friend, family member, or business colleague.
- A buyer can **empathize** with people in a story or examples of people struggling through events like those the buyer is experiencing.
- A buyer can **anticipate** events that will impact him or her personally.
- A buyer can **recall** events from the past and emotional turmoil that was experienced on a personal level.

In a recent *Psychology Today* article, Peter Noel Murray wrote, "Neuroscience tells us that the emotions associated with our judgments guide us in making decisions. Emotions and feelings are components of rationality in that they reveal what is important to us. When we are confronted with a decision, emotions from previous, related experiences affix values to the options we are considering. These emotions create preferences which lead to our decision."[6]

To stimulate emotions in B2B buyers, we must create a sense of urgency around "why change, why now, and why us?" Sellers can help forge the connection between experience and emotion by recounting trigger events, reviewing past situations, telling stories, and sharing examples.

How Can You Create Conversations to Drive the "Emotional Sell"? You can practice the "emotional sell" by conducting conversations that uncover both the business and personal benefits that buyers and users experience from the status quo. Include a strong dose of questions surrounding disappointments, uncertainties, risks, complaints, problems, threats, and anxieties. Often it will take only one or two questions to unleash a torrent of personal concerns surrounding the status quo.

Many years ago, a colleague was pressured by a sales representative to provide a simple model for selling. He answered with the old-adage: "Make 'em sick—make 'em well." While this may seem overly simplistic, it captures an important perspective on selling against the status quo. There is an emotional lever that drives action when a person feels sick or threatened. For example, most of us have experienced a toothache. We can identify with someone who wants treatment and wants it now. Everything else takes a backseat.

When a buyer has strong feelings or emotions associated with the status quo, the emotional sell is critical to any seller's success.

Using Stories and Visuals to Aid the Emotional Sell. A story accompanied by a visual aid is a powerful tool for the emotional sell. People remember stories and visuals more than they remember data. When crafted well and told skillfully with a visual, a story introduces several key ingredients to a business conversation.

- A story raises the interest level of the buyer and stimulates emotions.
- A story helps the buyer identify with a character of "action" (i.e., someone from real life who achieves an outcome through action).

- A story reveals a solution or new perspective to the buyer.
- A story and visual is far more memorable than graphs and charts.
- A story can convey a message or moral that justifies action.
- Great stories use similes and metaphors to amplify their point.

Stories and visuals make a powerful impact on customers. One really good story with simple visuals can answer many questions.

> John was trying to sell a new software package to the Chief Medical Officer of a mid-sized healthcare system.
>
> After doing his due diligence, meeting with all the stakeholders, and piloting the software successfully, he knew his challenge was to overcome the "cost of change" and "fear of blame and repercussion." In his meeting, John combined storytelling with a visual aid to appeal to the emotion and logic of the CMO.
>
> When they met, John told the story of a CMO in the southwest faced with similar challenges—the internal resistance to change, the fear of adapting to innovation, and the concern that the implementation would cost more in time that had been projected. When John completed his brief story, he walked to the whiteboard and wrote down three numbers. He then said, "I want you to remember 3 outcomes (See Figure 6–3)

4 Hours	$50,000	$5M

Figure 6-3: Three Outcomes

- 4 hours regained daily per physician
- $50,000 saved per physician annually
- $5,000,000 saved system-wide annually.

> The Chief Medical Officer got kudos from the CEO and BODs.

How Can You Build a Compelling Story? Storytelling is an art that requires skill and imagination. When combined with a visual, it appeals to emotion. Here are the major components that can help you build a compelling story.

- **Become a good listener**. Stories are everywhere—just listen and pay attention! People are telling stories on TV channels, YouTube, and radio stations. For sports fans, ESPN combines stories and facts 24 hours a day. Friends, neighbors, and colleagues are telling stories. As you listen, be analytic. What made the story interesting for you? How did the narrator build conflict? Resolve conflict? Convey their message?
- **Craft your message**. Every good story has a message or moral. What's the key takeaway for the buyer? Make your message simple and powerful. It must contain a one-line "call for action."
- **Know your audience**. Successful storytellers know their audiences well. What is interesting and motivating? Will the buyer identify with the protagonist in the story? Not every story works for every audience.
- **Create your hero/heroine.** Every powerful story has a main character (a protagonist)—a person faced with a choice.
- **Build conflict**. Your story tells of consequences your hero faces that are similar to the consequences faced by your buyer. The consequences should be realistic and important. (This is where you win or lose. If your story doesn't provoke emotions like fear, concern, and anxiety, then the buyer will tune out. This is the dramatic "build.")
- **Resolve conflict.** You've created dramatic tension. Now you must resolve conflict through action. What steps did your hero take to overcome the obstacle or resolve the problem? (This is where your story generates a whole new set of emotions—relief, gratification, happiness, pride.)
- **Frame the message.** This is where you deliver your message and the "call for action." Connect the hero's action to the situation faced by your buyer.

- **Add visual images.** Visual images can be a powerful force in creating a memorable message.
- **Test your story.** Few of us are born as storytellers. Storytelling is a skill that requires practice. Work on the core elements of your story. Simplify. Dramatize. Provoke. Have friends and business colleagues share their reactions.

Continue to "wordsmith" your narrative. Make sure your word choice is appropriate for the audience. Limit your story to one minute. After about 60 seconds your buyer's attention and interest can wander and wane. Don't let your story become an epic.

Create Differentiation

People buy for their reasons, not yours. In the B2B world, buyers purchase a product, service, or solution to achieve a business result that is often specific and measurable. Key Performance Indicators (KPIs) such as revenue per day, reduction in wait times by X%, or cost savings of Y% per pallet are typical results expected by buyers. Sellers typically help buyers see the business results through differentiation and proof.

Differentiation appeals to the logical side of decision-making. Differentiation means to stand apart and to be different in a way that is meaningful to each individual buying influence. Without differentiation, the status quo looks appealing, and the choice reverts to cost.

Differentiation helps the seller avoid commoditization. There is no such thing as a commodity. It is simply a product waiting to be differentiated.[6] Done effectively, the buyer sees your solution as providing a unique benefit to the buying organization. Frequently, companies differentiate through quality, delivery, service, or warranty.

Addendum 4 provides additional examples of differentiation.

1. **Is your offer/promise/claim UNIQUE?** With an entrenched solution or supplier, buyers will want to know what your solution can do that no one else's solution can do. Unique does not have to mean

you are the only one who can deliver a solution; you may be the only one who will align well with the buyer's desire or perspective, or your solution may simply be better.

2. **Is your offer/promise/claim RELEVANT?** Without relevance, buyers fail to see a connection between your proposal and the threat, problem, or opportunity that's "top of mind."

3. **Is your offer/promise/claim IMPORTANT?** You may have a great solution, but the problem or challenge is relatively low on the buyer's list of priorities. Your solution fails to "move the needle" on an issue of concern.

4. **Is there PROOF to support your offer, promise, or claim?** When you challenge a buyer's perspective, they may want evidence of your claim. Do you have test results, performance measures, testimonials, case studies, or references?

If your offering falls short in one of these attributes, buyers may find it easy to ignore or dismiss your proposal.

At the end of this chapter you'll find options for differentiating your product, your company, yourself, and the type of relationship you offer in competing with the status quo.

Break the Rules

The reality is that sellers often find themselves competing on a playing field that is heavily weighted in favor of the status quo. On any "apples to apples" comparison, the seller's product or solution is likely to involve startup costs, training issues, and time considerations that won't arise if the buyer decides to retain the status quo.

Far too many sellers craft a solution that is defined by the status quo. Essentially, they offer a solution that replicates the status quo in a faster, easier, and cheaper way. Don't replicate the status quo. Don't live with the playing field defined by the current supplier, product, or solution. That's a formula for failure.

In order to challenge the status quo, you will need to be bold and daring. Think big. Violate the buyer's expectations. Expand the pie. Here are two guidelines to keep in mind.

Don't think about your product versus their product—think about what you can do to exceed their expectations. Redefine the playing field. For example, if a company's current software solution links two departments, consider a solution that addresses enterprise connectivity. While more is not necessarily better, greater connectivity aids in strategic planning, financial oversight, speed to market, and accountability. Help the buyer understand the value of addressing tomorrow's challenges today.

A friend who sells CRM systems relates this story.

Story: The CRM Seller

After calling on the Sales Vice President of a mid-sized furniture distributor for several years, our friend finally gained the interest of his target. The SVP admitted begrudgingly, "Our CRM system is a bit antiquated, but it does what we need. I'm not ready to give up on it, but I am willing to listen to your ideas. Why don't you visit with our representatives and listen to their concerns? Truth is: they are the holdup. It took me forever to get them to enter data on a consistent basis. Now they don't want to go through the training and ramp up that would be associated with a new system."

So, our seller went about his discovery process. He talked to managers, sellers, marketing, and finance. Here's what he uncovered from his interviews.

Finance:	*"We need improved forecasting accuracy. Their forecasts are way off-base. It makes planning a real problem."*
Marketing:	*"Sales is always complaining about us . . . but we have no access to the CRM system. So, we have no idea what's going on in the sales funnel. How do they expect*

> us to create content when we don't know where opportunities are in the funnel?"

Sales Management: *"From our perspective, the CRM system is supposed to help us do our reports. We don't have time to coach and plan, and still compile weekly reports."*

Sellers: *"They told us the CRM system was for us—to help us know what activities are necessary to drive opportunities toward closure. Instead, the CRM system is all about keeping track of us. They should just put a monitoring device on our ankle."*

Our friend saw four unmet needs: improved forecasting accuracy, alignment between sales and marketing, automation of coaching and planning, and productivity. Rather than focus on an "apples to apples" comparison with their current CRM system, he focused on solving the four problems.

He won the sale, but he didn't contend with the current system. He used his discovery process to identify enterprise-level concerns that linked back to the CRM system. Could the existing CRM system address these issues? Possibly . . . with some upgrades. But our friend ignored the direct comparison of systems and focused instead on solving the strategic issues that were troublesome at the executive level.

In every sale, there is the opportunity to provide additional value that prompts buyers to question their commitment to the status quo. Top performers often mention:

- On-site training and updates
- Performance guarantees
- On-site personnel
- Financing options
- Free customization

- Web-based training and testing
- Joint development of an implementation plan
- The depth and breadth of their implementation team
- Proven results

Key Points to Remember

So where do you go with this mixture of neuro-science, logic, and traditional selling practices? How do you optimize your position and leverage the vulnerabilities of the status quo? Consider the following elements in building your sales approach.

1. The status quo can be a powerful, well-entrenched, internally supported competitive force.
2. Look for signs that the status quo is unbeatable as well as signs that buyers may be receptive to change.
3. Understand the buyer's perspective on the status quo. Are there performance issues, trigger events, or feelings that surround the current solution?
4. Top performers re-qualify the sales opportunity, calculate and share the cost of inactivity, and cultivate internal sponsors. They help the buyer manage the change process.
5. Social psychology tells us that we are two or three times more motivated to avoid a risk than to achieve a gain.
6. There are two parts to our brain. The logical portion demands evidence and proof of results. The emotional portion of our brain addresses safety and survival. It detests risk.
7. A good storyteller sparks emotion while educating buyers. When structured properly with a visual that shows a "before" and "after", it's memorable.
8. "Why now" messaging can help the seller transfer fear and risk from the new product to the status quo.
9. Sellers can differentiate their product, company, and themselves in many ways. One very effective way is for sellers to bring their ideas,

experiences, and perspectives to client encounters through stories and illustrations.

YOUR COMMITMENT

What is the one thing you will commit to doing differently because of reading this chapter? Please share it here or on a separate sheet of paper.

ADDENDUM 4: CREATING DIFFERENTIATION

Differentiate Your Product/Service

Sales professionals can differentiate their product or service in many ways, as shown in Figure 6A.

Examples that Differentiate Your Product or Service

Product Attributes/Features	Perceived Quality	Purchase Price
Technology	Reliability	Usage Cost
Performance	Efficiency	Total Cost of Ownership
Uniqueness	Safety	Location
User Friendliness	Convenience	Brand-Name Value
Design	Style	Warranty
Durability	Availability	Repair Record

Note: These are just a few examples and are not meant to be an exhaustive list.
Figure 6A: Product Differentiation

Top performers are adept at illustrating how their product exceeds the status quo. This approach works well with individuals who will use or supervise the use of the product. However, it may not resonate with whomever is going to authorize the expenditure of funds.

When differentiating product quality, savvy sales professionals often cite the length of the product's warranty, compared to the competition. The implication is that the product is better designed and will require less maintenance and repair. This message resonates well with engineers, users, and materials management.

Price differentiation is the least sustainable option for an outside supplier. There will always be costs associated with implementation, training, and ramp up that make a new solution more expensive than the status quo.

Differentiate Your Company

Successful sellers can also differentiate their company to gain competitive leverage as shown in Figure 6B.

Examples that Differentiate Your Company

Product Portfolio	Consistency	Technical Support
Reputation	Customization	Service Installation
Industry Leadership	Convenience	Terms and Conditions
Ordering Options	Training	Return Policy
Inventory Levels	Pre-Sale Support	Management Flexibility
Ease of Doing Business	Post-Sale Support	Loyalty Programs
Delivery Schedule	Service Policy	Size and Financial Strength

Note: These are just a few examples and are not meant to be an exhaustive list.
Figure 6B: Company Differentiation

Company differentiation is often based upon the firm's overall size and financial strength. Sellers often highlight industry leadership as demonstrated by the depth and breadth of their product portfolio and their history of innovation and patented technology. Additionally, sellers emphasize the company's pre-sale and post-sale support.

Many providers tend to focus on their industry record, client list, convenience, specialization, and their reputation for service.

Differentiate Yourself

Top performers understand that they are a key component in the customer's buying decision. So, they differentiate themselves, as shown in Figure 6C. This is especially important for organizations that sell a service. For example, consulting firms have no easy way of articulating the differences between two firms. They must sell their talent and their ability to provide an insight to uncover an issue the prospect doesn't see. In a recent study, the Corporate Executive Board (now CEB-Gartner) reported that 53 percent of 5,000 buyers said it was the seller's experience, not the product, service, solution, or organization that drove customer loyalty. The sales representative offered unique valuable perspective on the market.[7]

Sources of Personal Differentiation

Preparation	Honesty	Organizational Skills
Expertise-Competence	Courtesy	Project Management Skills
Experience: Personal and Industry	Accessibility	Reliability
Product Knowledge	Communication Skills	Responsiveness
Business Acumen	Innovation-Creativity	Follow-Through
Integrity	Eagerness to Please	Empathy
Providing Insights	Likeability	Patience
Listening skills	Intelligence	Learning Ability

Note: These are just a few examples and are not meant to be an exhaustive list.

Figure 6C: Personal Differentiation

Successful sales professionals bring expertise, business acumen, and insight or perspective to every client encounter. They encourage their clients to see a new reality—a new possibility that is better than their existing condition. Top performers provide a measurable value to their clients by sharing perspective and insight.

A seller's expertise may provide a broad and rich view of the business milieu and an understanding of the headwinds and tailwinds.

Appease the Need for Proof

It's natural for sellers to demand proof that a seller can deliver on their promises. Proof instills confidence in their purchase decision and reduces the risk of a mishap. In Figure 6D, we show some common forms of proof or documentation.

Examples that Demonstrate Proof

References	Financial Calculations: ROI, NPV, Payback and TCO	Testimonials
Case Studies	Published Research	Guarantees
White Papers		

Figure 6-D: Forms of Proof

Chapter 7

Surviving & Winning Beauty Contests (RFP Processes)

"Almost always, the RFP itself offers great clues as to whether or not a response can result in success."

Tom Searcy, author of *RFPs Suck!*

To most sellers, the Request for Proposal (RFP) process is a form of supplier terrorism practiced by many Procurement offices. We have an image of several Procurement agents sitting around the table chuckling at some impossibly complex requirement they have just added to the RFP. One snickers, "They'll never see this one coming." Another adds, "And with a due date of four days after Christmas, they'll never see their families until January."

We know these characterizations are wrong and undeserving, but many requests do appear highly restrictive and designed to limit the seller's ability to understand the buying organization, and they require submission dates that make the sellers' lives miserable. Do they go to school to learn these tactics? No, and there are steps sellers can take to improve their positioning and level the playing field. Consider this sales initiative with an automotive assembly plant.

Story: The Automotive Assembly Plant

Several years ago, a U.S. automotive assembly plant was preparing to take their foodservice program "out to bid." Carlos, a sales representative in the corporate dining division of a global foodservice company, had been preparing himself for this opportunity for several years. He met all the key stakeholders, spoke frequently with Procurement, and visited with the union representative. Carlos took copious notes on every one of the coffee shops and cafeterias, fleet of food trucks, and army of vending machines. Those were the facilities necessary to serve more than 4,200 employees working three shifts.

The foodservice program was massive, complex, and disorganized. The food trucks were owned and operated by six different vendors who showed up when they wanted and the weather permitted. The service at the coffee shops and cafeterias was poor at best. The health department representatives were afraid to eat in the cafeterias.

The Senior Vice President for Operations had instructed the head of Procurement, "Bid out the three cafeterias, and leave the food trucks and coffee shops alone. Let's keep ourselves off the front page of the newspaper, on the good side of the union, but what I really want is our fair share of the spend that goes on in our facilities. See what you can do to get me a big chunk of change. Under no condition are we going to mess with the vending machines, coffee shops, and food trucks!"

Previously, the head of Procurement (Joanna) had met with Carlos. She thought, "I remembered that he had some good ideas for driving revenue, and he knew our facilities better than I do. I wish I could find my notes."

When Carlos read through the RFP, he was very disappointed. Without the revenue potential from food trucks, coffee shops, and vending, it was going to be impossible to provide the automotive manufacturer any commission. In fact, Carlos was concerned that his boss might see the whole project as too risky to bid. The RFP was quite specific in prohibiting the revenue from food trucks, coffee shops, and vending machines.

He met with Joanna from Procurement. She was sympathetic but explained that there were political and community issues. The Senior Vice-President-Operations didn't want to provoke any negative public relations, since they were beginning contract negotiations with the automotive union.

Carlos' Regional Vice President gave him a call that raised a glimmer of hope: "I've got an idea that just might work. Let's get together and see if we can find a way where both sides can win and keep Procurement from disqualifying our bid."

After they met, Carlos followed their game plan and executed their script to precision. On the due date specified in the proposal, Carlos arrived at Joanna's office. "Joanna, this box contains our proposal for the business specified in the RFP. Make no mistake: this is our *only* proposal. I think you will be disappointed in the financial benefits—but we are severely limited by the restrictions in the RFP. However, I do have a second box for you. It is not a proposal . . . it is 'reading material' that you may find very exciting. Whether you read it or not is up to you."

A week went by without a response. A second week passed without a call. At the end of the third week, Joanna gave Carlos a call. "Carlos, that was very clever on your part. You knew that I couldn't resist looking through your 'reading material.' Everyone is impressed by your diligence and attention to financial detail. Your 'reading material' gave us a roadmap for improving the foodservice for everyone while making a good financial return. We ran your plan by the union team, and they loved the innovations. This could provide us with a bargaining chip in labor negotiations, as you pointed out in your road map. My boss had a very short directive for me: 'Let's make this deal with Carlos happen.'"

Carlos' Regional Vice President summarized their RFP strategy: "The whole point of an RFP is to give customers choices. Let's give them the best options we can. Whether they choose to break their own rules—that's their choice."

Seller's Challenge: *Build a Powerful Strategy to Overcome the Limitations and Biases of an RFP Process*

The RFP process may be disruptive for even the most experienced seller. Develop a strong sales plan that recognizes the biases and limitations of the process yet maximizes opportunities to provide the buyer with a complete view of the value of the seller's products and/or services. The seller needs to recognize when to comply dutifully, object respectfully, or act disruptively.

To develop an effective sales strategy when the buying process is structured around the formal solicitation of proposals, sellers should give careful thought to what they need to know about the RFP process, how to calculate their probability of winning the sale, and the key elements in building an effective proposal. Consider the approach taken by Carlos in this story.

Not all RFP processes are flexible. Some are structured to ensure that the buying organization will have their needs met, while others are designed to ensure the buyer can justify a decision that has already been made.

IS THE RFP INVESTMENT WORTHY?

To begin, let's take a closer look at the types of RFPs, the harsh realities of RFP processes, and the caution signs that should alert sellers to reconsider their participation in the process.

What Are the Types of RFPs?

An RFP is a legal proprietary document prepared by the buying organization to identify and attract the best vendor(s) to supply them with the desired product, service, or solution.

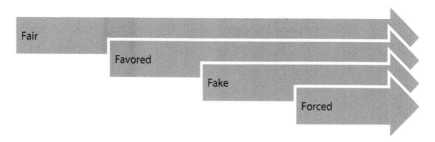

Figure 7-1 The Four Types of RFPs

The Four Types of RFPs

- **Fair RFP:** The RFP identifies specifications and requirements essential to meeting the buying organization's needs. The fair RFP is intended to create an equal footing for suppliers and a format for presenting solutions, products and services.
- **Favored RFP:** The RFP is written in a way that favors one company over all others. The RFP process may be a smoke screen to create the impression of fairness while providing an advantage to one seller over others.
- **Fake RFP:** The buying organization is satisfied with their present vendor but uses the process to satisfy government or industry standards and statutes.
- **Forced RFP:** The RFP process is designed to compel the current supplier to provide favorable price discounts or other concessions for fear of losing the business.

There can be good reasons for RFPs. Often the process can serve one or more of the following seven needs of a buying organization.

1. Assist the buying organization in differentiating products that meet performance specifications from those that don't. It also allows them to see "what's out there" when they may not have stayed current with new products, technology advancements, etc.

2. Enable "side by side" price comparisons among suppliers for a reality check against what their pricing assumptions may have been.

3. Limit or contain selling activities that threaten to interfere with the formalized buying process and timeline.

4. Provide leverage in negotiating improved financial conditions with existing or preferred vendors.

5. Ensure compliance with governmental and industry standards for awarding contracts.

6. Provide free consulting or a customized road map for solving a problem.

7. Create a safety net. With several people involved, no one person will be blamed if the wrong product or service is selected.

It would be difficult to imagine how companies in some industries (like aerospace, construction, education, defense, and IT) could ensure product quality, integrity, and safety without the intensive product scrutiny afforded by an RFP process.

While RFP processes are meant to create an evaluative environment that is "fair for one—fair for all," some companies create review processes and requirements that favor one supplier over others. The evidence may be subtle, such as a deadline that favors the existing supplier. Or the RFP may contain performance specifications that are excessively restrictive.

Harsh Realities of RFP Processes

While the RFP process gives the appearance of fairness and equality, the harsh reality is that most are neither fair nor equal. The RFP is meant to differentiate and exclude with criteria that is often subjective, not objective. The process is intended to help technical advisors or technical specialists say, "No," and provide a basis for limiting purchase options. Consider ten additional harsh realities.

1. RFPs are often used by organizations to validate the decision they have already made and to drive the price lower by their preferred

vendor. Organizations don't change easily. Sometimes, there are internal political dynamics in play, whereby the credibility and reputation of certain stakeholders in the buying organization may be tied to historical decisions that have already been made.

2. Buying organizations are measured and rewarded based on the unit price and savings they secure, rather than if the RFP meets the needs of customers (e.g., Total Cost of Operation, impact to outcomes, patient safety, etc.).

3. The win rates tend to be very low for new, small, or mid-sized companies. To win the business and overcome the buyer's real or perceived cost of change, these types of organizations may have to surrender significant discounts or provide free products or services.

4. Price is heavily weighted in most product comparisons.

5. The buying organization may have a preferred supplier list that is hard to crack.

6. It can be expensive and time consuming to craft a comprehensive response to an RFP.

7. Many buyers are less interested in buying and more interested in getting free consulting services.

8. Many decision makers read only select parts of the written proposals, typically dealing with subject areas that are already highly familiar to them.

9. Some RFPs are pre-sold by someone, and the RFP process simply provides the appearance of a level playing field.

10. RFPs that are heavily weighted on cost savings comparisons rather than value serve to commoditize the market.

Caution Signs in the RFP Process

When one or more of the following caution signs appear, carefully reconsider any sales opportunity involving an RFP process.

- The buying organization has never used a formal RFP process but now appears to favor this form of evaluation.

  Caution: The buyer may be attempting to protect a preferred supplier. They may also be "checking the box" to show that they have undertaken an RFP exercise.

- The timelines and submission dates don't permit adequate preparation.

  Caution: The current supplier may be urging the buyer to pose deadlines that will hinder competition.

- The RFP includes unnecessarily stringent product specifications that appear to favor a single supplier.

  Caution: Determine who benefits by restrictive specifications.

- The RFP denies the seller access to the various stakeholders involved in the process.

  Caution: Explore who really makes the decision. Is someone "vetting" options and making recommendations?

- No one seems to know who authored the RFP.

  Caution: A competitor or consultant may be providing boiler-plate information.

- The RFP embraces a range of products that normally has different buyers.

  Caution: Internal reorganization may underlie process changes. Discover how power may have shifted.

- The RFP doesn't include a bid meeting or formal opportunity to raise questions and explore answers.

  Caution: Ask for a meeting with the buying team to resolve questions and explore customer needs.

- The RFP does not seem to represent the criteria/weighting the customer has indicated is most important to them.

  Caution: There is a disconnect between the customer and Procurement. Greater customer engagement may be required, otherwise price will become the deciding factor.

- The buying organization is using an online software RFP package that requests that all costs associated (e.g., labor, burden, overhead, materials used, gross margin, etc.) are provided in a detailed format.

  Caution: This is a slippery slope for suppliers, because this information can be used to leverage a lower price or justify going to a competitor.

Myths of the RFP Process

RFPs can be complex, demanding, and oblique. Sellers can find themselves so entangled with forms, templates, and appendices that they fail to question whether their response does their product and company justice. It's vital that sellers get past five myths of the RFP process:

Myth 1: The RFP process outlines how the customer will buy.

Reality: Normally the RFP describes very little about the overall buying process. The RFP may provide insight into the purchaser's scorecard system, but it may not clarify who will review their proposal and what weightings they will apply to key criteria.

Myth 2: Those who manage the RFP process are the decision-makers.

Reality: That's not true. They may have the ability to exclude sellers who fail to adequately demonstrate product performance, but they can seldom award a contract or purchase order. A possible exception could be countries with governmental mandates.

Myth 3: Proposal guidelines are binding.

Reality: Proposal guidelines are meant to afford an easy "apples to apples" comparison, but that doesn't mean the guidelines are binding (governmental agencies may be a lone exception). The seller's challenge is to differentiate their product based on value. Proposal guidelines shouldn't interfere with the seller's ability to present their case. We have seen guidelines or rules change mid-stream or at the end to ensure that customers get what they want.

Myth 4: **Standardization promotes fairness and equality.**

Reality: Procedures are meant to standardize, NOT impair. Steps that are taken to standardize often limit a seller's ability to share additional research or testing, customer testimonials, references, and case studies. For example, the RFP may require that a product price be listed in a specific format. What if total cost of ownership (TCO) is a more appropriate measure of cost than product price? Procurement presents the optics of fairness and equality; however, they work for the customer, and they are not an impartial adjudicator.

Myth 5: **It's best to provide only the information required.**

Reality: The required format for a response to an RFP may limit a seller's ability to tell the whole story of a product or solution. Offer them content that they didn't request but can't resist. Consider providing more than one proposal, or alternate bids, if you have additional options for the customer, or feel you know their needs better than as they were defined in the RFP process.

DEVELOP A PLAN TO WIN THE "BEAUTY CONTEST"

Sellers should resist the temptation to view the RFP process as the full buy-sell cycle. The challenge sellers face is to plan their sales strategy early, connect with all buyers and stakeholders, convey a powerful value message that differentiates the seller's solution, and keeps the communication lines open no matter how restrictive the RFP.

1. **Differentiate Your Proposal at the Executive Level**. Connect with executive-level decision-makers before distribution of the RFP. If possible, help to shape or write the RFP so you can "lay mines" for

your competition. Confirm that your value messages resonate with decision-makers and differentiates your solution from the competition.

2. **Understand the Buying Process.** Ask: Who will participate in the decision-making process? Who is responsible for the ultimate decision? Who will use the product or service? Who might resist or be a blocker in this process? Why now? What is the compelling business reason? What are the chances the buyer will stay with the status quo? Who is the incumbent? Who is managing the RFP process? Is it Procurement or the buying team? Do you know anyone in the buyer's organization?

3. **Discover the Buyer's Decision Criteria.** Probe to understand how the buyers intend to scorecard proposals—including specific criteria and percentages. Do they have Key Performance Indicators (KPIs) that are vital to their decision? How do they calculate key measures? How important are these value metrics compared to cost savings? Does it appear that a competitor shaped the RFP? How has your existing provider addressed these needs? What are the problems that the buying organization is trying to solve?

4. **Demonstrate Your Capabilities.** Show capabilities that surpass the scope of work but are relevant and valuable to the buying organization. What insight into the buyer's customers can you provide?

5. **Probe Your Competitive Position.** Secure feedback on your competitive position and the relative strength of your competition. Is there a preferred supplier? How well entrenched is the status quo? What would motivate change?

6. **Assess Buyer Risk.** Probe to understand all concerns that may stall or undermine the sales process. If the product doesn't perform as claimed, who (in the buying organization) is most at risk? Focus on the stakeholders who shoulder the greatest risk and reassure them that there are no risks with your solution.

7. **Verify Timelines and Submission Dates.** Some RFPs have timelines that are "moving targets," making it difficult to manage a selling

process. What steps will occur after the RFP has been submitted? How many suppliers received the RFP? When will a decision be made?

8. **Develop a Proposal Strategy**. What steps must be taken to render a compelling proposal by the required submission date? Would each decision-maker see value from their perspective in your proposal? What resources are required by the selling organization? Will you have an opportunity to present your proposal to the buying team? Who will be your Subject Matter Experts (SMEs) when you present to the buying team?

9. **Keep Messages Flowing**. Once you have established an open channel to executive-level buyers, keep messages flowing. Keep executives apprised of recent test results, additions to your client list, testimonials, or case studies. Continue to reinforce value messages. Do not retreat to your office and put your cell phone on mute so you can write your proposal. Continue to sell!

10. **Qualify the Opportunity**. The temptation with a formal RFP process is to assume that the buying organization will make a good partner. The buying process will shed light on the buying organization's culture and values. Are the buyers likely to be long-term customers? Are they driven by price alone? Are there future opportunities to sell additional products? What is the cross-sell or up-sell opportunity? Can you schedule a telephone call or meeting with the process leader? Why was your firm selected to receive the RFP? What do they know about your company's products and capabilities?

How to Calculate Your Chances of Winning

Your chances of winning the RFP increase with your understanding of the buying process and quality of the relationship you have within the customer's organization, as shown in Figure 7–2.

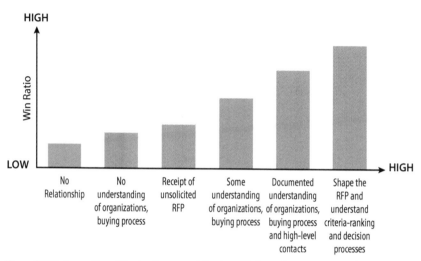

Figure 7-2 Understanding of Buying Process and Quality of Relationship with the Organization

Build Your Response Around What Matters to Buyers

Behind all the narratives, the forms, the legal language, and technical specifications, there are buyers who harbor fears and concerns. Consider what matters most to buyers. Craft messages (in the proposal and presentation) to reassure buyers in the following five ways:

1. **Your proposal is safe.** It reduces downside risk for the buyer, ensures product availability, and demonstrates product integrity. In other words, it produces the results buyers desire.

2. **Your proposal is affordable.** You have taken steps to make the proposal a responsible investment with a documentable return.

3. **Your team is prepared.** Your team includes the technical expertise and experience to implement, train, coach, and trouble-shoot problems on-site.

4. **Your team is responsive.** Current clients are willing to share how your team confronts challenges.

5. **Your company is committed.** There is clear executive-level support from your organization. Your organization is committed to executive involvement in periodic performance reviews and contract discussions.

6 Ways to Increase Your Win Rate in Responding to an RFP

To increase your win rate in responding to RFPs, give thought to the following six ways to boost your success. In our experience with companies across a variety of industries, the following six steps are potential keys to success.

1. **Know your market niche.** The probability of success may decline as much as much as 20% when sellers stray from their market segment.
2. **Say "no" to more RFPs than you say "yes."** A good rule of thumb is to say "no" to twice as many as you say "yes." An exception to this would be if RFPs are normal in your industry or mandated by law.
3. **Partner with a small company that has unique capabilities**. Choose partners carefully. Some small companies may bring a vital key to strengthening your proposal.
4. **Assess receptivity to change among buyers**. Throughout the sales process, continue to qualify buyers based upon their history, interest, and appetite for change.
5. **Gain early commitment for a presentation time**. Most buyers read only a few sections of the proposal. Given the time, dollars, and resources required to submit a proposal, the very least the buyer can do is commit to a presentation time.
6. **Know your customer's customer.** At the end of the day, every buyer is attempting to serve a customer. What do you know, or what can you learn that will enable the buying organization to better serve their customer?

GUERRILLA TACTICS: KNOW WHEN TO BREAK THE RULES

Breaking the rules of an RFP process can have a definite downside. Your proposal can be disqualified or devalued. You must make a candid assessment of your position relative to the competition and determine whether it's possible to win the opportunity without breaking the rules. Consider the merits and penalties associated with the following situations.

1. **Unfavorable or Unrealistic Submission Dates.** We've all experienced an RFP process that had unreasonable deadlines. In some situations, the timeline is designed to favor the current supplier. Before you commit your time and resources to a competition that puts you at a disadvantage, consider voicing your concerns.

    Recommended Action: When time is an enemy, you may wish to protest the proposal's submission due date. Most timelines are arbitrary or designed to meet the needs of the buying organization. For example, some purchasing agents have been guilty of setting a submission date immediately following a holiday, which makes it almost impossible to comply without working through the holiday. You should review deadlines and raise objections at the bid meeting with written follow-up. Remember: you are not just submitting a proposal—you are investing time and corporate resources.

2. **Denied Access to Primary Decision-Makers and Key Stakeholders.** If you can't access key decision makers, how can a buyer make an informed decision? How can you convey value?

    Recommended Action: When access to decision-makers is denied during much of the proposal preparation period, you may wish to submit written objections with full explanations of the information needed. Executive decision-makers may not be informed of all restrictions. If needed, "create noise" that can be heard by the people you can't contact directly.

3. **Price Is the Primary Decision Criterion.** This is no longer a selling process—it's a bidding process.

   Recommended Action: When price is the primary criterion, and the format required for the proposal permits only a price quote, change the forms, alter the computations, and make your own schedule. You may choose to include an addendum that provides a more complete financial analysis than price alone—perhaps a business case with Total Cost of Ownership, ROI, or Payback. Don't expect Procurement to quantify your value if you can't do it yourself.

4. **The RFP Is Overly Restrictive in What the Seller Can Provide or Explain.** Often RFPs can be unreasonably limiting. You're not able to present a business case that would substantiate your claims of financial value. There is no way to provide test data to support the value of a higher-priced product.

   Recommended Action: When your "hands are tied," consider crafting a short compelling case and incorporating a narrative wherever appropriate. Some sellers have been successful in submitting multiple proposals (including separate price quotes), sliding scales, or incentives for large orders or bulk purchasing. This is very effective when the Procurement process doesn't seem to match the true needs of your customer.

5. **The RFP Understates the Scope of Work.** On occasion the authorship of the RFP has fallen into the hands of someone who doesn't grasp the complete scope of work that must be undertaken to complete the mission presented in the RFP.

   Recommended Action: You may consider "expanding the pie," even submitting a proposal or solution that is well outside the defined scope of the RFP. If possible, link your solution to vital, executive-level initiatives that may cause a Procurement executive to "think twice" before tossing your proposal.

6. **The RFP Is Unclear About Terms, Conditions, and Pricing.** This can be subtle evidence of a bias in favor of the current supplier. After all, who is likely to understand the normal terms and conditions for conducting business? The current provider!

   Recommended Action: You may want to submit in writing your request for clarification or make price, terms, and conditions contingent upon clarification. This can be helpful if you are seeking an extension.

7. **Lack of Responsiveness to Seller's Concerns.** While there can be explanations for unresponsiveness, it's a clear sign that you don't have clout with some of the buyers involved.

   Recommended Action: When the technical buying group is unresponsive to your concerns, make sure you submit written objections and copy the relevant executive if it won't get you disqualified. In some markets, communication goes only through a designated contact. However, regulations are starting to be less restrictive. Another effective tactic is to create a "groundswell" of support among users who see value in your product or solution. Encourage users to become vocal advocates behind the scenes.

In determining your readiness to pursue an RFP, consider your own frame of mind. Are you approaching the process as a respondent or as a seller? Did you anticipate the RFP and use the time before distribution to connect with stakeholders and differentiate your product/solution? Based upon your preparation (or lack of preparation), you may wish to reassess whether the opportunity is winnable and worth the expenditure of resources and time.

When to Say "No"

Saying "No" is not a sign of weakness—it's a frank assessment that this particular buying process is not a suitable investment of your time and resources. Here are six situations that may warrant an emphatic "No."

Situation 1: The RFP process requires an excessive amount of customized work. The buying organization may be looking for free consulting services. Draw a line separating what is appropriate and what is too much.

Situation 2: The buyer has failed to provide a reason for change. If you can't detect a trigger event or performance failure that would warrant change, you may be the "stalking horse" in a price negotiation with the current supplier. Beware: the status quo may be entrenched and unbeatable.

Situation 3: The time frame (including submission date) is too restrictive. If the submission date is unfavorable or unrealistic, then don't waste time and resources. Respond with a polite but firm ultimatum. If they really want your participation, they will amend the timeline.

Situation 4: The buying team, Procurement officer, or primary user is highly critical and demanding. Is this going to be an account that everyone wishes would go away? We've all sold accounts that created more headaches than revenue. Is this a manageable account?

Situation 5: Your product, service, or solution does not meet the requirements for the RFP. Sometimes the "fit" just isn't there. Don't waste time and resources. Move on!

Situation 6: The RFP appears to be written for your competitor, and the resources required to answer the RFP are greater than the anticipated revenue and profit.

How to Say "No"

Whenever you decline to participate in an RFP, it is important to keep the door open for future opportunities. Always start your response by thanking the company for the opportunity to participate. Tell them you would like to work with them, just not on this specific RFP.

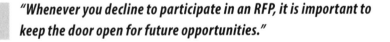

"Whenever you decline to participate in an RFP, it is important to keep the door open for future opportunities."

This is easy if your solution isn't a good fit for their requirements. If you think the RFP doesn't reflect the unique capabilities of your product, then tell the customer. As an example:

> *"While our organization would love to respond to your RFP, we are concerned that you will be buying technology that will soon be obsolete.*
>
> *Our solution provides a platform for add-ons as technology evolves as well as provides users with Artificial Intelligence for improving throughput, cleaning, and preventative maintenance. With that in mind, we reluctantly pass on this RFP. We would, of course, like to be considered for future opportunities to work with your organization."*

If you feel the RFP doesn't allow you access to key people, you should make that clear as well. As an example:

> *"While our organization would love to respond to your RFP, we feel that we don't have a complete understanding of your current solution and the project's technical, operational, and financial objectives to provide a meaningful response. For that reason, we will not submit a proposal to this RFP. Of course, we would like to be considered for future opportunities to work with your organization."*

Afterthoughts for Sellers

An RFP process poses both threats and opportunities. Smart sellers say "No" far more often than they say "Yes." An unexpected RFP can take you out of the field for a week or longer while usurping corporate resources. Thoroughly consider what's to be won or lost. We hear too many sellers (especially new additions to the sales force) say, "That's my job. I'm supposed to make these tough sales." No. Your job is to make your number . . . your responsibility is to make the right call.

RFP debrief meetings can be very useful. Sellers should ask for them after a loss or a victory. You will always learn something valuable in these meetings. Try to get a key stakeholder to come to the meeting (maybe your coach) to make sure it is not just a price-based discussion or an exercise in unrelated excuses.

Often RFPs ask for conditions that are unreasonable under threat of disqualification. For example, they may require 120-day payment terms. Make sure you are not agreeing to conditions that clearly penalize the seller.

If conditions like a 120-day payment term are stipulated, take some time to ensure you are not agreeing to things that benefit only the buyer.

14 Key Questions to Consider

1. Does the RFP present a level and equal playing field? Buyers may just want to confirm a decision already made, pressure their incumbent for a lower price, or gain free consulting.
2. Is this a winnable opportunity, or is the status quo or current supplier entrenched with strong internal support? Check your probability of success.
3. Do you understand the business goals and decision criteria?
4. Is your solution a good fit for the buyer?
5. Does the buying group have a history of selecting the lowest price?
6. Do you understand the competition and their relationships to the buyers?
7. Do you have the resources to respond to this RFP in the time allowed?
8. How entrenched or impenetrable is the "status quo"?
9. Is the financial return worth the investment of time and resources?
10. Are there opportunities to continue accessing buyers and connect with the executive buyer?
11. What materials, documents, case studies, business plans, or testimonials will help you succeed?
12. Are there channel partners or other small vendors who offer a unique capability or product that would elevate your chances for success?

13. Are there "top2top" opportunities to connect a senior executive from your organization with the executive buyer?

14. Do you have a strong relationship with the client or executive buyer?

Key Points to Remember

1. There are four types of RFP: favored, fair, fake, and forced. Know the difference.

2. Many RFPs are neither fair nor equal. Procurement works for the buyer—they are not an impartial mediator of process.

3. Sellers should proceed carefully with an RFP when one or more cautions signs appear.

4. Don't allow myths around the process to get in your way of winning the RFP.

5. There are ten keys to developing a winning plan for selling a proposal. Use them all.

6. Always calculate your chances of winning.

7. Build your RFP response around what matters to buyers.

8. There are 6 ways to increase your win rate with RFPs.

9. Know how and when to use guerrilla tactics with an RFP.

10. Know when to say "No" to an RFP.

─────────────── **YOUR COMMITMENT** ───────────────

What is the one thing you will commit to doing differently because of reading this chapter? Please share it here or on a separate sheet of paper.

Chapter 8

Inside the Black Box

Harsh Realities of Selling to a Committee

"Consensus is an opinion or position reached by a group as a whole."
Anthony Iannarino—author of *The Lost Art of Closing*

ommittees are the mysterious black boxes of the sales universe. Sellers often assume they know what's inside the box, only to find that it was not at all what they suspected. The word "committee" is often used to cloak the secrecy of the buying process. One individual's "committee" is another's team or group. Within a company a committee is a group of people appointed by someone of authority to investigate, analyze, recommend or resolve an opportunity, problem or threat. When executives are questioned about how they are going to render a buying decision, you may hear some of the following organizational double-speak.

"I'm going to have a group of department heads look at our options."
"I've got a team of users that will guide us."
"When we get to that point, I'll bring together a project team."

"I'll start with Procurement and then get feedback from department heads before getting the final 'OK' from Finance."

Do any of these comments help you define a committee's role in the buying process? The responses are so vague that it's difficult to know whether this is an *ad hoc* group, a formal committee, a board, or simply a list of people who must "sign off" on a decision before a purchase is authorized.

Many committees or boards are a formal part of the organizational structure. They may work under such titles as Quality Assurance Team, Board of Directors, Buying Committee, New Product Committee, Technology Selection Committee, Evaluation Committee, Project Board, Steering Committee, and others. Within a company a committee is a group of people appointed by someone with authority to perform a service or function. Committees may be charged with one or several of the following objectives:

- To reduce risk factors associated with decision-making
- To increase collaboration from various organizational groups
- To ensure compliance with governmental or industry regulations,
- To promote standardization
- To mobilize internal support that would ease and speed implementation
- To balance decision-making objectives for hitting financial goals and delivering on end users' needs

Several years ago, an account manager told us a story that illustrates how important and difficult it is to gain an accurate understanding of a buying committee, its membership and its decision-making process.

Buying Committee Story: "Who's on First?"

This story, told by a global sales executive for a major IT company, reminds us of the great Abbott and Costello routine called "Who's on

First?" (For readers who have never heard the great comedic routine from 1953, check it out on youtube.com.)

The sales executive was launching a sales campaign to rework the data centers for a potential customer who was dissatisfied with her current supplier. While our account manager was confident that his team was well positioned with the executive buyer, he was concerned about the size and complexity of the committee that was appointed to review proposals and guide the purchasing process. He knew the names of some (but not all) of the nine- or ten-member committee. Also, he was forewarned by the executive buyer that additional members may be added to the committee.

To cover his bases, the account manager put together a group of specialists and assigned each selling-team member to one or two buying-committee members. The account manager developed a communication plan through which sellers interviewed, built rapport, and exchanged insights with their buying team members. The selling team was tasked with obtaining two vital pieces of information: "who" will participate and "how" will they decide. Easier said than done!

When the global account team reassembled a week later to compare feedback from the committee members, the leader found the reports to be confusing. Here are some responses from the committee.

- Two participants predicted "the group will likely assemble in the next month . . . but there could be delays."
- One member was convinced "the group is just a formality and will endorse whatever the boss wants."
- Another member pointed out that she "would like to be on the committee but hasn't heard anything."
- Two additional members argued "there is nothing wrong with our data centers today. We should leave well enough alone. What are they thinking?"

Yep! "'Who's' on first." "'What's' on second." "'I don't know' is on third."

Seller's Challenge: *Develop and Execute a Committee-Focused Winning Sales Strategy*

Discover the various interests as well as the professional and political differences among committee members. This may require a team on the selling side that delves into the mindset of stakeholders on the buying side. Without this, the disparity within the buying committee could undermine a sales strategy that strives to engage, inform, and unify them behind a single solution.

What should a seller know and do to sell effectively to committees? It's critical for sellers to understand the complexities and realities of committee decision-making, how to research multiple stakeholders, deploy teams of sellers, control unexpected threats, and handle tough challenges. In this chapter, we'll take a close look at how top performers handle these challenges while they manage consensus-driven committee processes.

THE COMPLEXITY OF THE SELLER'S CHALLENGE

Recent surveys indicate that the number of stakeholders involved in purchasing decisions is growing significantly. It is not unusual for sellers who were used to balancing two or three buyers in the past to now be challenged with far more complex groups of five, six, or seven committee members. The complexity of the selling process grows with the complexity of the buying process; it must be adjusted to address the number of members on the buyer teams, groups, and committees.

How Is the Complexity of Buying & Selling Growing?

Buying committees, whether formal or *ad hoc*, increase the complexity and difficulty for the seller. Here are four problem areas facing sellers.

- Sellers may be faced with selling to many individuals who hold diverse opinions and needs that conflict with others.
- Committee members often act differently in a group than when they are approached individually.
- Committee meetings are often influenced by internal political issues that have little to do with the seller's product.

- Sellers are outside of the buying organization, so it can be hard for them to know how each committee member will measure success. Buyers may want to arrive at a decision that supports their individual function within the organization. Through coaching and guidance, sellers can make meetings and presentations relevant for each buying committee member, so the committee can reach a collective "Yes."

Five Harsh Realities of How Committees Operate

It's not just the committee size that disrupts the buying and selling processes. Consider the following realities that plague a committee's decision-making.

1. **All committee members are not equal**. It would be a mistake to assume that all parties get to vote or have equal say in the buying process. Some committee members may be included only for a specific function such as explaining test results or offering legal guidance on contract terms.
2. **Information is not always shared**. Some members hoard relevant information or distribute data at the last minute for political reasons.
3. **Different committees employ different decision processes**. Some may decide by vote, others may require a consensus or formal "sign off" before authorizing a purchase.
4. **Committee members may not share a common sense of urgency surrounding the buying process.** Those charged with using, managing, or operating the solution are likely to share the greatest sense of urgency.
5. **The easiest decision for a committee to make is the decision to "do nothing."** It requires the least effort and (many times) involves the least risk. "Do nothing" is often your most challenging opponent. Simply put, some members don't want to take on the extra responsibility and work that comes with implementing a new solution. The larger the committee, the more likely the decision dynamics will lead to a "stalled" or "no decision" verdict.

It can be a real wake-up call for a seller who expects colleagues in the buying organization to read the proposal and make a quick decision.

HOW CAN SELLERS GET INSIDE THE BLACK BOX OF COMMITTEE DECISION-MAKING?

Top performers rely on four key elements (see Figure 8–1) when they prepare and execute a strategy that wins the sale: research the committee and stakeholders, deploy the selling team early, control threats to the presentation, and be prepared to handle tough challenges. Each of these will be described below.

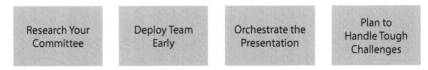

Figure 8-1 Four Key Elements for Preparing and Executing a Committee Strategy

Research Your Committee

Committees are composed of many people within an organization and occasionally a select few from outside the organization. A Governing Board for a not-for-profit hospital in a local community is a good example. Each member of the committee has a different title, area of focus, business, personal objective, personality, and preference. People often act differently in a committee meeting than they do when meeting with a sales professionals one-on-one. Within a group, the leader or one influential person can change the dynamics quickly and unexpectedly. One person with specific expertise (e.g., legal) can shift the group's position quickly.

Before engaging a committee, the seller may find it helpful to conduct a discovery process that answers many of the following questions. Sellers may not always get the answers, but the discovery process can be invaluable for building a strong sales strategy.

Sellers should consider the following questions and topics when building their understanding of the "who," "what," and "how" of committee decision-making.

Committee Composition and Size. A great starting point is to first learn who will participate and how the committee was assembled in the first place.

- How many people are on the committee?
- What are the names and titles of the individuals who serve on the committee by function (e.g., department, area of focus, etc.)?
- Who does the committee report to in the organization?
- What are the requirements to be on the committee?
- Who created the committee and assigned its members?
- Is the committee a "standing" group or an "*ad hoc*" committee? (This speaks to the committee's experience as a working team. For example, an *ad hoc* committee may not have any collective experience in managing a complex purchasing decision process.)
- Who is the chairperson of the committee? How long has this person been the chair?
- Are there any sub-committees within the committee? If yes, what are the sub-committee names, how many people serve on them, and what are the names and titles of the people who serve on them?

Committee Meeting Frequency. Almost every committee creates a calendar for meetings and conference calls. This can predict a lot about the speed and time frame for decision-making.

- How often does the committee meet?
- Does the committee publish a meeting calendar for the year?
- Where (within the facility) does the committee meet?
- Are the committee meetings open or closed to suppliers?
- Does the committee publish minutes of their meeting? Are the committee minutes confidential?
- Does every committee member attend each meeting?

Committee Charter. When establishing a committee, executives will often write a cover memo that outlines expectations for the group, specifies implementation timelines, and explains the impact of the pending decision on corporate goals.

- Does the committee have a charter, and how was the charter created?
- How long has the committee been in existence?
- What information can the seller provide to the committee that would be of value?
- What are the committee's mandates or priorities, such as budget limits or implementation schedule?

Committee Process. A committee's process refers to how the committee will conduct business, including the notification of suppliers, issuance of a Request for a Proposal (RFP) or Request for Qualification (RFQ), product testing, or essential requirements and specifications.

- What issues are most important to the committee?
- How was the decision-making process managed the last time this product or service was purchased or negotiated? Does the committee have the mandate to improve upon prior processes?
- Is there a deadline or "buyer's window"?
- Will the committee use a scorecard or formula to compare solutions or weigh various items?
- Do any of the committee members have an opinion on the seller's product, service, or solution versus a competitor and the status quo?
- Besides the seller, what other solution is the committee considering? Is the status quo an option?
- Does the committee allow suppliers to present to the committee? If yes, how much time is allocated?
- Will there be a "blackout" period, during which vendor engagement will be restricted?

Committee Authority and Decision Dynamics. Knowledge of a committee's decision dynamics can help a seller better understand the challenges they are facing. It's easy for sellers to make wrongful assumptions about how decisions will be made or the influence of certain stakeholders.

- How does the committee decide?
- Are the decisions of the committee based on quality, price, and/or other factors?
- What criteria and weighting does the committee use to decide?
- What is the weight of each voter on the committee?
- What is the voting process?
- Is the committee's decision binding and final?
- Who are the most influential members of the committee?
- Who on the committee, if anyone, has veto power?
- How often does the committee vote yes for a new product or service without eventual implementation of that decision?
- What company has been most successful with the committee?
- What measure(s) is the committee expecting from the successful vendor?
- Once the committee decides, what happens next?
- If 100% of the committee members do not agree, how is a decision made?
- If the committee vote is split 60–40 for the change, is the committee committed to the change?

Deploy Team Early

Many sales professionals receive a wake-up call when they find out they can't do it alone. The number of buying-committee members becomes too daunting, and there isn't enough time for them to connect to all stakeholders without professional help and support from the selling organization. It shouldn't be surprising that help is required to cover all bases early enough in the buying process to win the award. Here are some helpful tactics for the seller.

- **Assemble a Selling Team.** Commit early to assembling a selling team. Include technical specialists and other sales assets as they are necessary. Think beyond product specialists, and consider adding team members with consulting skills and extensive operational experience. No need to swim without a life preserver!

- **Craft a Playbook.** Develop a "mini playbook" that links value messages to each buying persona. Cite terminology, Key Performance Indicators (KPIs), and critical concerns for each persona. Modify your playbook after each round of interviews with buying committee members.

- **Design/Implement a Communication Plan.** Build and execute a communication plan that includes interviews, email messages, and PowerPoint key points. Assign members of the selling team to committee members with like interests and expertise.

- **Build Executive Connections.** Enlist executives from the selling organization and push "top2top" connections as appropriate. Use a playbook to help prepare executive sponsors for conversations, and debrief them afterwards.

- **Share Team Insight.** Conduct weekly debriefings to share information, gain competitive insight, and conduct a straw poll to see where team members feel they stand relative to the competition.

- **Manage "The Vote."** During sales interactions with buying-team members, try to get an understanding of how they will vote. Develop a strategy that leverages the influence of those who appear to be voting in your favor over those who lean toward your competitor. Keep track of how this strategy unfolds during the decision-making process. Each meeting with a competitive vendor could sway your supporters to reconsider their vote.

- **Engage Your Champion(s).** Ask your Champions or sponsors to be proactive and articulate your value. Be sure they can describe a risk-mitigating strategy, and explain your position or price.

- **Create a Social Media Presence.** Use appropriate social selling tools (Twitter, Instagram, LinkedIn) to create and sustain a presence; be a contributor and thought leader—NOT a seller. Make yourself known as a source for insight and as an objective contributor who promotes and sustains dialogue.

Orchestrate the Presentation

Committee meetings are often executive "stews" that combine people with different skills, backgrounds, and decision-making styles to render buying decisions that have different financial, operational, and political implications for each executive. That's a formidable playing field for even the most skilled seller. It's vital for presentations to be customized for the group at hand. It's not about the product; it's about what the product does for a specific organization and the seller's ability to document his/her claim.

Most sellers give presentations to committees frequently. Presentations can range from a fifteen-minute Q&A to a multi-hour comprehensive review of a company's response to an RFP.

Unfortunately, many presentation styles speak more to what the seller feels is a safe and comfortable format than to what will resonate with the buyer. There are three key objectives for every committee presentation:

- Make it *relevant.* Make it about them.
- Make it *fascinating.* Bring valuable insights to share.
- Make it *engaging.* Connect each committee member.

Consider fourteen fundamentals or best practices for planning and delivering a memorable presentation to a committee of buyers.

1. **Customize Your Message.** In the weeks prior to a presentation, a seller often conducts interviews or sales calls with members of the buying committee. When doing so, the seller should focus on capturing each buyer's highest priority need or benefit. They should record what the buyer says as precisely as possible and confirm the statement with the buyer. It's best if they make a point of referencing the buyer's name with his or her statement.

One seller had a quote from each member of the buying committee printed on a poster and mounted on the wall. Each buyer (by name) was associated with a quote that described a high-profile need. During the presentation, the presenter referenced her conversation with each buyer, the buyer's quote, and how the solution addressed each buyer's stated need. Buyers love recognition. Build your credibility by investing time and hard work to prepare a solution that works for the buying organization.

2. **Own the Room.** Space is a major factor influencing the outcome of a presentation, especially one attended by five or more members. Always inspect the room or presentation area well in advance. How much wall space is available, and how will you use it? Where are the electrical outlets? Is there adequate space for presenters to move or participants to congregate? What are the audio-visual requirements of the area? A boardroom may be great place for a meeting but a horrible place for a presentation. Even though you may be presenting in the customer's office complex, the audience expects the presenter to "own" the room.

Ask yourself, "How can I use this space to convey my message?" Can you use wall space to display visuals or graphics? What visuals might prompt your audience to believe that this presentation is important to you and your company? Is there enough space for smaller groups to break out for hands-on time with the product?

Story: Refreshment Services

A new sales representative in the refreshment services industry was preparing her presentation for a company that wanted a variety of beverage and food vending machines. The presentation was scheduled for a small conference room in the customer's office complex. It felt claustrophobic. After having lunch with a friend in Marketing at the buying organization, the new sales representative changed the presentation to a large room and (with the help of Marketing) staged seating and conversation areas for coffee breaks and lunch.

She reasoned that it wasn't about the machines—it was about the coffee-drinking experience and the warmth and inclusiveness of the area. The buyers were greatly impressed. This changed the presentation from a competition of equipment to a test of which company could create the experience the customer wanted to achieve. Big win!

3. **Combine High and Low Technology.** Here's the bottom line: don't fall in love with your standard PowerPoint presentation. Audiences like visuals, pictures, and wall displays. Meeting participants have seen their share of PowerPoint presentations and have an appetite for a variety of different formats. Combine the use of whiteboards, flip charts, models, and displays, with streaming video and PowerPoint.

4. **Craft an Agenda that Addresses Member Issues and Interests.** An agenda sets the tone for the meeting and shows your professionalism. Consider the following introduction. It lets you know if the buyer's priorities have changed since your last meeting and ensures your understanding of them. It also demonstrates flexibility: *"The purpose of our meeting today is to discuss the findings from our discovery process. Is there anything else we should add to our agenda before we begin?"*

   By asking the audience to rank the objectives or list desired outcomes, you involve them, communicate the importance of their input, and confirm your understanding of the situation they face. Be sure to stay on track and control everyone's participation so the meeting doesn't become lengthy or drift off the key message.

5. **Engage the Audience.** In developing the presentation, presenters should consider how and when to engage the audience. Keep the audience participation succinct and focused, but don't delay it until the Q&A period at the end. Involve the audience with specific questions that help expand key points. Everyone likes to feel important and hear their name referenced among their peers. Use this opportunity to address influencers and get confirmation of what matters most.

6. **Tell a Great Story.** Research shows that well-told stories are far more memorable than hard data. But a poorly told story can kill a

presentation. Good stories have several characteristics in common. They are short—less than a minute long. The stories are relevant to the buyer. They tell of a situation the buyer is experiencing or of an experience with which they can identify. A good story demonstrates that the seller understands the buyer. Stories build rapport and credibility. They should have a hero who is challenged by a seemingly overwhelming situation. The hero (or heroine) should be an individual who appeals to your buyers—someone they can identify with (not a seller). Clearly explain how your hero's choice of your company's solution resolved the problem the hero was facing. Finally, articulate the measurable or documentable benefits to the hero/buyer. Good storytellers can turn off the projector, tell a one-minute story, and win a sale.

7. **Plan a Surprise.** If you surprise your attendees, they will reward you with their attention because they'll wonder, *"What else does he/she have planned for us?"* Surprises don't need to be magic acts or elaborate stunts. They can be a hidden or unexpected picture or graphic. We've seen a banner unfurled to reveal a theme, a table of logo items prepared for the customer's organization, and an artist's rendering of a remodeled hospital entry. Each became a memorable feature of the presentation. A simple surprise could be to place tent cards around the table with everyone's name on them. It's unusual and memorable. The point of a surprise is to illustrate the selling organization's willingness to invest additional effort to earn the buyers' attention.

8. **Monitor Two Emotional Barometers.** There are two key emotional gauges that can help the seller determine whether the presentation is on track. First, the seller should be focused on driving down the buyer's estimation of risk. Is the presentation reducing the buyer's "fear of failure?" The presenter needs to understand the sources of risk (as perceived by the buyer) and plan counter-measures to alleviate the buyer's fear. Second, determine the buyer's sense of urgency.

During any presentation, the seller must help the buyer recognize the pain and cost associated with no change.

9. **Keep It Simple and Powerful.** The presenter should keep the presentation short, simple, and relevant to the buying team. It's far better to focus on two or three key differentiators than five or six. Follow the "rule of threes" and limit each PowerPoint slide to three key points. Consistently link a threat or opportunity to a solution that drives the buying process.

10. **Consider the Order of Presentation.** "If you and a competitor are presenting back to back, you should go first because you will shape your potential customers' perception and create biases that will put your competitor at a disadvantage. Researchers refer to this as the *primacy effect*, which describes the brain's tendency to be more influenced by what is presented first than by what is presented later. If there is some time between presentations (more than a week) you should go last. This is because memory of your competitor will fade with the passing of time, while your presentation will be fresh in the buyer's minds."[1]

11. **Plan for the Unexpected.** Let's face it: stuff happens! Plan contingencies for the following eventualities.

    • **The meeting starts late**. The meeting starts later than expected, which means you have less time for the presentation and questions. **Recommended Action:** For an hour presentation, plan for 45 minutes. Have a "game plan" if time runs short.

    • **Unexpected stakeholders attend. Recommended Action:** Ask them to introduce themselves and define their objectives for the meeting.

    • **New topics or interests surface during your introduction. Recommended Action:** Add them to the agenda and pre-determine which member(s) of the presentation team will handle the topics or interests.

    • **Technology issues surface.** Examples could be the lack of a projector, a burned-out bulb, or a laptop failure. **Recommended Action:** Always have backup equipment available.

- **Team members drift off message.** Team members may lose the attention of the audience with way too much technical detail or inappropriate comments like, "Of course, we can throw that in" or "Absolutely we can sharpen our pencil." **Recommended Action:** Practice your presentation in advance and agree on who will make decisions.

- **The audience reacts aggressively.** At times, stakeholders can view presentations as opportunities to showcase their expertise or interject disruptive insights. **Recommended Action:** Offer to discuss the concerns with the stakeholder "off line." Reassure them that controls are in place to manage the situation. Or, reposition the comment by saying, *"This raises a broader issue of _____. Let's focus on the greater threat and our plans for controlling the downside."*

12. **Practice Your Presentation.** Conduct one or more "practice" presentations and interactions. Don't allow anyone to say, "I'll do this," or "I'll cover these three slides." Demand that everyone execute his or her portion of the presentation as if the customer were present. This is how you hone your presentation and execution.

13. **Discuss Next Steps.** At the end of every presentation, you should share an "advance" or "call to action" that describes the next best steps to move forward collaboratively. Committees are slow-moving enterprises that require guidance and direction—otherwise processes are likely to stall.

14. **Plan a Follow-Up.** Within 24 hours of your presentation, we recommend that you send a follow-up email to committee members and address the following points.
    - Reiterate the business issues
    - Stress the urgency of action
    - Reinforce your capability and your product's link to the business issue
    - Document the agreed upon next steps

Use the following as a guideline:

Dear Committee Chairperson,

We appreciated the opportunity to meet with you and the committee on (insert date) to better understand your problems, opportunities and threats, and your urgency for change. Our presentation had a twofold purpose. First, we crafted a customized solution that will achieve your business objectives by providing you the ability to do _____. Second, we developed a "road map" that will optimize productivity. For us to move ahead, we agreed that the next steps would be (insert agreements, letter of intent, etc.).

I will call you in one week to discuss any unanswered questions and begin the process to formalize our partnership.

Plan to Answer Tough Challenges

Committee meetings can become competitive forums for stakeholders to demonstrate their expertise, voice opinions, and support special interests that have little or nothing to do with the buying task at hand. Often committee members will "push back" on a claim, point of analysis, or recommendation as a way of gaining attention or appearing to be "tough-minded." A common tactic is to press the presenter with challenging or unreasonable questions. Sellers or selling teams would do well to prepare answers to tough questions like these.

1. "Specifically, what can your solution provide us that your competitors can't?"
2. "If we give you a 'yes' today, would you be willing to reduce your proposed price by X%?"
3. "Describe a time when a significant problem surfaced. How did your company attack and solve the problem in a timely fashion?"
4. "How many product recalls have you had in the last three years?"

5. "If you don't perform to the level of your ROI, are you willing to adjust our payment model to compensate for the shortfall?"

6. "Would you provide us with a couple of client references—that we could call this afternoon—who would share any problems or challenges that surfaced during implementation?"

7. "What guarantees can you provide us on repairs, downtime, and delays?"

8. "Would you be willing to reimburse us for all of our costs incurred if your product requires service during the warranty period?"

9. "In this industry, what previous customers did you lose in the last two years and why?"

10. "Undoubtedly there are times when you lose new business opportunities to a competitor. Why did your prospects choose a competitor?"

11. "What alternative financial models or payment systems have you offered prospective customers?"

12. "We have a narrow window to achieve full implementation of your solution. What resources has your organization identified to ensure an error-free ramp-up, including all training and testing?"

13. "One reason we have resisted your products (and others in the market) over our own internal solution is that, when things go wrong, we've got talent on-site 24/7. Why would we want to give up that safety net?"

14. "Your company (like your competitors') has a planned lineage of product revisions. What product rollouts can we expect from you over the next three years for the group of products we are considering today?"

15. "We've seen a lot of you over the last two months. We appreciate your interest, but why haven't we met any members of your executive team?"

HOW TOP PERFORMERS WIN BY BUILDING CONSENSUS

Often sellers find themselves building a sales strategy based on a common, but faulty, assumption. They assume that the decision will be made by "majority rule." That sounds reasonable, doesn't it? "Majority rule" is the governing "golden rule" of our decision-making universe. But it doesn't always work out that way. In many businesses, "consensus rules." It may be a company's way of creating political stability among factions or ensuring a decision that is acceptable to all.

What Are the Hidden Challenges of "Consensus Buying"?

"Consensus buying" poses several important questions for sellers:

- Does every buyer have veto power?
- What recourse does the buying committee have if one member dissents?
- How can sellers build consensus around their proposals?

There are three "hidden" challenges sellers should consider when building consensus.

1. **Committee Size:** Many committees never reach a buying decision. There is a strong negative correlation between committee size and likelihood of reaching an agreement.[2] As committee size increases, the probability of reaching a purchasing decision drops sharply. With a committee size of approximately 5.4–6 members, the probability of reaching consensus on a purchasing decision falls to 31%.[3]

2. **Impasse:** Committees need help in building consensus early in the decision-making process, not later. Often committee members find themselves divided over the scope and the need to change. "Why change?" "Is it worth the expense, time, and aggravation?" "Is this a top priority?" "How will this play out politically?" A study by the Corporate Executive Board found, "Consensus often falls apart before sales reps even arrive on the scene."[4]

3. **Politics:** Consensus-driven committees can be challenging political landscapes. Members may fear losing credibility with others, landing on the wrong side of a political issue, or being blamed for product

or service failure. So, while a member may favor one position over another, they may be unwilling to advocate that position in group discussion. The CEB (now CEB-Gartner) study found that approximately 50% of the participants who held a willingness to buy were unwilling to publicly advocate their preference.[5]

Tips for Surmounting Obstacles with Consensus-Driven Committees

So how should sellers proceed when faced with these obstacles? Building a sales strategy for consensus-driven committees may take sellers in a direction that is contrary to common practice.

- **Gain Early Access**. A *Harvard Business Review* article pointed out that many sellers get involved too late to influence consensus.[6] They arrive with a "choose me" pitch as committees are selecting a solution. Committee members need to confront and surmount obstacles to consensus early in their discussions.

  Recommended Action: Sellers need to provide insight or perspective on the problem and solution process. Committees are not looking for a pitch—they want brand-neutral insight. What lessons can you share from the experience of other customers as they struggled to make decisions?

- **Motivate and Prepare Champions.** Conventional wisdom prompts sellers to find an influential Champion or advocate who will build support for the seller's position. That may be a challenge for consensus-driven committees. Finding and utilizing Champions, advocates, or mobilizers in a consensus-driven process may be difficult, because they may perceive political or career risks.

  Recommended Action: Help Champions have the confidence and insight to contribute to the discussion process. Share content that's supplier-neutral. Don't expect sales skills from Champions—prepare them to offer relevant observations and ask probing questions.

- **Build Common Language and Insight.** A seller's focus should be on building and sharing a common perspective that links stakeholders to one another. Sometimes decision-makers have common interests but divisive language; their terminology blocks them from connecting.

  Recommended Action: Sellers should create a language "map" and help stakeholders recognize common interests.

"The best way to build customer consensus isn't to do a better job of connecting individual customer stakeholders to the supplier but to connect more effectively customer stakeholders to one another."[7]

WHY *"AD HOC"* COMMITTEES ARE GREAT SELLING OPPORTUNITIES

As the Latin phrase suggests, *"ad hoc"* can refer to a group, team, or committee that is established for a specific situation or task. It is not a "standing" committee or a formal part of the organization's structure.

Why would an *"ad hoc"* committee present a great selling opportunity? First, let's look at "standing" committees. Most formal committees have a structure, process, timeline, agenda, and established leadership roles. Standing committees usually have a chairperson (or co-chairs) who leads the meetings and reports to an executive responsible for the actions or decisions rendered by the group. They have established meeting dates and times. Everyone knows how the committee will decide or what they will recommend. It's easy for any competitor to discover quickly the "who," "what" and "when" of the committee.

That's not the case with most *ad hoc* committees. These groups are far less structured. They are less rule-bound and more informal. Here's what it means for the seller:

- **Greater Member Access**. It may be easier to access members because there are no formal rules restricting buyer-seller contact.

  Recommended Action: Sellers should take advantage of the situation to connect early and frequently with all committee members.

- **Limited Experience/Product Knowledge.** Several committee individuals may not fully understand the task, process, or product choices and could benefit from the seller's insight and experience. Also, sellers should help buyers understand the value and differential of their product.

  Recommended Action: Sellers should help these members understand the seller's company, history in the market, and success with customers.

- **Your Experience Is Needed.** The committee chair or leader may be interested in briefing documents, articles, and test results that raise the knowledge base of the committee.

  Recommended Action: Sellers should begin providing impartial, industry-relevant articles and materials that can be distributed. Help the committee leader with "dos" and "don'ts" of the process. Advise the leader of financial options and legal language they may wish to adopt. Offer "boilerplate" narrative for RFPs and contracts. Sellers can also offer to help with the scope of work.

- **Greater Receptivity to Change.** Fewer committee members have a pre-established position on the competitive choices or a bias against change.

  Recommended Action: This presents an excellent opportunity to help members forge an initial perspective on products and the unique benefits and strengths of your product or solution. Seller should be "planting seeds" that can be nurtured throughout the process and harvested as the committee formalizes.

Key Points to Remember

There are key takeaways for sellers to consider when building an effective sales strategy for committees.

1. Committees are now an integral part of the buying process, and they are not easily circumvented.
2. Selling to a committee is distinctly different from selling to several diverse stakeholders.
3. Committees are formed to reduce the risk factors by involving more people in the selection equation. Much of their discussion may focus on identifying sources of risk and systems for mitigating risk.
4. Top-performing sales representatives spend significant time learning about the various buying committees and asking questions to improve their understanding of how culture and politics influence decision-making.
5. When faced with a large committee, sellers should ask for help, including technical personnel, executives, and other sales assets as needed.
6. Some committees have a decision-making process that requires consensus. Getting to a consensus can be challenging for many sellers. Buyers need help early in the buying process to unify committee members.
7. Finding and utilizing Champions, advocates, or mobilizers in a consensus-driven process may be difficult, because they may perceive political or career risks.
8. "*Ad hoc*" committees can be an excellent selling opportunity. Sellers should get to the leader and members early and find ways to help them define and implement their decision process.

--- **YOUR COMMITMENT** ---

What is the one thing you will commit to doing differently because of reading this chapter? Please share it here or on a separate sheet of paper.

ADDENDUM 5: CHECKLIST FOR PREPARING TO SELL TO A COMMITTEE

Validate composition and size

- ☐ Who are the members?
- ☐ What challenge does size pose?
- ☐ Are there any sub-committees conducting research, testing, or background work?
- ☐ Are there any specialists, consultants, or technical experts assisting the committee?

Check committee meeting schedule

- ☐ When is the committee meeting?
- ☐ Who is managing the committee process?
- ☐ Are committee meetings open to suppliers?
- ☐ Does the committee publish minutes of their meetings?

Determine committee charter

- ☐ What mandate was given for the committee?
- ☐ How long has the committee been active?
- ☐ What role, if any, did the committee play in the status quo?

Identify committee process

- ☐ How will they decide? Vote? Recommend? Report?
- ☐ When do they expect a decision?
- ☐ When do they expect implementation?
- ☐ Is there a discovery period?
- ☐ Are there restrictions to member contact?
- ☐ Does the committee have a timeline and deadlines?
- ☐ Where is the committee in their buying process?

☐ What information does the committee request or require from the suppliers?

Determine committee authority and decision dynamic

☐ Once the committee decides, what's next?
☐ Will they issue an RFP?
☐ To whom in the organization does the committee report?
☐ Is the committee conducting research?
☐ Is the committee using a supplier scorecard?
☐ Who on the committee has veto authority?
☐ Is the committee's decision final?
☐ If 100% of the members do not agree on a solution, how is a decision made?
☐ What other products or services are they considering?
☐ Is staying with their current solution an option?

Chapter 9

Frenemies

Partnering with Procurement

"The key for you as the salesperson to remember is that even though the purchasing department's number one objective is to save money, this doesn't mean they are out to attack you on price."

Mark Hunter—author of *High Profit Selling*

All too often, sellers view Procurement as the dark force that obstructs the selling process. They are the "black hats" that delay or stop sales. They are viewed as the commandoes of commoditization. Some sellers believe Procurement is so obsessed with price discounts they turn a "blind eye" to obvious product value. Consider setting aside this arcane misperception of today's Procurement executive, and replace it with a strategy that builds an environment of collaboration.

Many sales professionals are surprised at the growing power and influence of Procurement in the buying process. Don't be! If sellers compared notes with their counterparts in other industries and in other countries, they would understand the increasing importance and expanding relevance of Procurement.

In this chapter, we are using the term "Procurement" as a generic reference. In some firms, the more appropriate term may be purchasing, contract management, materials management, supply management, global supply-chain management or strategic sourcing. You get the point.

In our view, the term "Procurement" embodies the strategic focus of the role and its importance to the organization. Procurement is a business-management function that ensures identification, sourcing, access, and management of the external resources that a team or department needs to fulfill its strategic objectives for the organization, its stakeholders, and its customers. Procurement's expanded role is the result of several factors: increased global competition, the relentless pursuit of cost savings, and the outsourcing of more functions within the value chain.

Many of Procurement's skeptics within the sales ranks are sellers who have had great success in selling to individuals within an organization but outside of Procurement, such as project managers, design engineers, surgeons, or department directors and managers. In other words, they have succeeded in breaching "silos" where one influential individual can authorize or strongly influence the purchase of a specific product or service. These seasoned sales professionals, while competent and skilled, have often failed to step back and observe the "sea change" that has occurred within their target organizations and Procurement's rise in importance.

Story: Selling Office Furniture

Jerry joined a large, family-owned-and-operated office-furniture dealership as a new sales representative when his predecessor, Ben, who had been with the company for 10 years, left to take another position. Jerry wanted to make a good impression with a quick sale, so he decided to call on the Vice President of Procurement for the largest manufacturer in their city. He had read in the newspaper that they had broken ground on a new facility and figured they would need plenty of new office furniture. As Jerry was planning for his sales call, his boss told him not to set his expectations too high because the Vice President of Procurement was known to "eat suppliers for lunch" and cared only about the lowest price.

Jerry heard the input but didn't let it influence him. When he met with the Vice President of Procurement, he made the sales call all about the buyer and his needs. He didn't discuss product at all. He brought insight to the Vice President by asking about what type of work would be done in the various areas and if they specified ergonomic furniture that would reduce stress and workplace-associated injuries. You can guess what happened. Jerry won the business.

Not everyone has a success story like Jerry's. As you read this chapter, you will see that, in some situations, there is no win-win relationship with Procurement. One thing is certain, however—if you view Procurement as the enemy, they will perceive it, and your path to success will be long and arduous.

Sellers Challenge: *Develop a Sales Strategy that Incorporates Collaboration and Minimizes Conflict and Dispute with Procurement*

In building a sales plan, sellers are challenged to create a road map that allows the seller or selling team to communicate freely and openly with Procurement while accessing strategic buyers. Recent trends have seen growth in the power, size, and complexity of the Procurement function. Sellers are challenged to work collaboratively with Procurement to maximize contact with buyers, lessen pressure for price concessions, and convey a product's full value to the buying organization.

Sellers would be wise to keep in mind that Procurement professionals often possess strong operational, technical, financial, and/or clinical backgrounds in their industries. They are trained negotiators. Think about the last point for a minute. In a typical organization, Procurement negotiates several times each day. The average sales professional negotiates several times per month or quarter. Who do you think has the advantage?

The ascension of Procurement varies by industry. For example, within a multi-national firm like Apple, Procurement is vital to new product releases. Within hospitals and healthcare systems Procurement has risen from the "back room" to the C-Suite. This has occurred at the expense of individuals and department heads who in the recent past made purchasing decisions. While these individuals remain a part of the buying process, they have less authority and influence. They still have a voice in the buying process, but they are now one among several.

In many industries, sellers find it necessary to re-evaluate their network of relationships and understand the answers to three questions:

- As I prepare my sales plan, what do I need to understand more fully about the role of Procurement, their systems, and their processes?
- Who from Procurement should I know better?
- What measures (financial and operational) are they using to assess the value of products and solutions?

In this chapter we'll explore how Procurement is changing, arcane myths about Procurement, and what benefits Procurement uses to compare products and solutions. Also we'll take a close look at tactics used by top performers to engage and collaborate with Procurement.

HOW IS PROCUREMENT CHANGING?

Prior to the economic downturn in 2007, companies often established capital budgets and thresholds for decision-makers by department. Today, several executives may share oversight on any given purchasing decision. These senior managers often entrust Procurement with greater responsibility and control over the buying process. This is reflected in seven trends:

- **Business Process Outsourcing:** Procurement organizations are actively engaged in establishing relationships with business-processing-outsourcing service providers and outsourced manufacturing partners. Procurement also manages these strategic relationships on an ongoing basis by carefully monitoring the performance of suppliers.
- **Leadership of Digital Transformation:** Procurement may play a leading role in transforming the enterprise to the digital age. Working in close collaboration with IT, operations, and other functions of

the organization, Procurement may be actively engaged in implementing new digital technologies such as robotics, data analytics, the Internet of Things (IoT), and cyber security.

- **Expanded Size and Specialization:** Many organizations have broadened the function of Procurement to include purchasing processes previously handled by department heads. To accommodate the change, they've increased the staff size and added product specialists or specialty buyers with deep experience in products or services.
- **Direct Connection to the C-Suite**. To give Procurement a greater command and voice in decision-making, dotted lines to the C-suite have become direct reporting lines. In some organizations, Procurement reports to a Vice President of Finance or Operations.

> *"To give Procurement a greater command and voice in decision-making, dotted lines to the C-suite have become direct reporting lines."*

- **Preferred Supplier Status**: Many Procurement teams are scorecarding suppliers to identify "preferred" providers that meet established criteria. For new or smaller suppliers, this presents a significant challenge.
- **Quota-Driven Supplier Negotiations**: To secure the best products under the most favorable conditions, Procurement executives are challenging their team to meet or exceed financial, performance, and service requirements.
- **Managing Business Benefits:** Procurement is often tasked with validating and reporting business benefits such as Internal Rate of Return (IRR), Return on Investment (ROI), Payback, and Net Present Value (NPV). Increasingly, Procurement leads enterprise business transformation. In the past, this was done by the Chief Financial Officer (CFO). Now they are the "tip of the spear" for efforts to achieve enterprise-wide cost savings related to merger-and-acquisition activity or strategic cost-reduction efforts.

The Changing Lens

The lens through which Procurement manages each buying process is changing. Procurement is shouldering a greater load, and the timeline for high-priority projects is tighter than ever. If we approach Procurement as an opponent or an undesirable critic, we are likely to find ourselves shut out of the purchasing process and closed off from valuable communication. Consider traditional differences between how sellers think and how Procurement executives think, as shown in Figure 9–1.

How Sellers Think:	How Procurement Thinks:
"I'd like a quick decision."	"This needs to have a thorough evaluation."
"I need to recycle my strongest, most persuasive dialogue for these guys."	"I'm tired of slick dialogue; show me the performance data I can rely upon."
"I've built strong executive relationships; they know my solution's value."	"Senior management likes these guys but wants me to provide hard evidence."
"These guys haven't even read my proposal that addresses planned benefits and projected value."	"These guys haven't even created a business case that provides measurable and convincing evidence of ROI and Payback."
"I hope we can make this simple. What one concession can I make to close the deal?"	"I'm not sure where to begin with these guys, so I guess we'll have to go over all aspects of the deal."
"I don't know what Procurement really wants other than a cheap price."	"If I can't find a compelling benefit, I guess I'll have to go back to price."
"My proposal is far superior to my closest competitor."	"If we can't get a strong deal with them, we may have to stay with the status quo and review the situation next year."

Figure 9-1 Mindset of Sellers and Procurement

What Functions Does Procurement Perform?

Procurement performs six core functions. Each one is central to Procurement's role, which is "to facilitate and enable the organization it supports in achieving its vision, mission, and goals."[1]

1. **Coordinate a buying process that engages stakeholders:** This may include communicating with stakeholders, soliciting concerns, polling for preferences, establishing agendas for meetings, and formulating timelines or "buying windows."

2. **Identify specifications, expectations, and requirements:** Often Procurement works with "users" to establish product specifications. They may deploy specialists to evaluate test results and conduct product comparisons. Procurement may require or create a business case that focuses on KPIs established internally.

3. **Source the product or service:** Procurement representatives will turn to their preferred supplier list to convey RFPs, RFIs, and RFQs. They may check credentials, require references, and explore service history.

4. **Negotiate the price, terms, and conditions:** Procurement may not be the exclusive negotiator, but they have a strong voice about when, what, and how the negotiations will proceed.

5. **Contract with one or more suppliers:** Working with the legal team, Procurement may influence contract provisions.

6. **Follow up with each supplier to ensure timely delivery or implementation of products and services:** Part of the expanded role of Procurement is to assess how well both the supplier and product met the expectations and requirements of the buying organization.

7 MYTHS ABOUT PROCUREMENT

These commonly held assumptions about Procurement share at least one commonality: they are either misleading or mythical.

 "Procurement pays attention to what senior leadership requires. Take a close look at the initiatives sponsored by the C-Suite."

Myth 1: Procurement's primary concern is to push down cost!

Reality: Procurement pays attention to what senior leadership requires. Take a close look at the initiatives sponsored by the C-suite. While cost-containment efforts are always appreciated, that may be less of an issue than coverage, global capabilities, safety, or durability. Cost containment and pricing are not the same issue. Product price is only one element in cost containment.

Myth 2: Procurement prefers to be combative instead of collaborative.

Reality: Procurement is often viewed as combative when they create a roadblock or don't immediately issue a purchase order. Sellers should not confuse concerns with being combative. Most Procurement personnel, especially those in leadership, are tactful, professional, and collaborative. They didn't get to a position of leadership by being disrespectful or difficult when working with suppliers. The seller can influence the relationship with the buyer through early engagement, education, pricing options, and a collaborative negotiation process.

Myth 3: Procurement is just a gatekeeper.

Reality: Think of Procurement as guardians and protectors of company resources instead of gatekeepers. This is a subtle but important change in the way a seller should approach Procurement. In many organizations, committees are making decisions, and the person leading the committee is often from Procurement.

Myth 4: Procurement equals Purchasing.

Reality: Procurement is really the art and science of Supply Chain Management. It's a planned and measured approach. It includes every activity from the acquisition and supply of goods and services to the disposal of goods and services no longer needed. Supply Chain Management involves setting policies and strategy, and it delivers measurable financial results. Purchasing defines and performs the tasks essential to buying. They handle requisitions and manage deliveries at the right price.

Myth 5: **Procurement is an obstacle for other business functions.**

Reality: Procurement works with "doers" so they can design or perform their work better, faster, cheaper, and with less risk. The perception of Procurement stalling the "doers" in the organization— i.e., those who design or perform the work—is a myth.

Myth 6: **Strategic sourcing by Procurement equals sole sourcing.**

Reality: Most Procurement organizations want more than one supplier, to reduce their risk. What if their sole supplier went out of business or was acquired by another company? Every organization that purchases critical components identifies the risks associated with being tied to one supplier.

Myth 7: **Procurement has all the leverage.**

Reality: Most sales professionals believe this myth because they have never walked away from a deal. Too often, sellers comply and concede so quickly that they never see the influence they can have on Procurement. Consider how much simpler Procurement's job becomes when they can work with suppliers they know, products they trust, and services that meet their needs.

IMPLICATIONS OF PROCUREMENT'S SUPPLIER-SEGMENTATION STRATEGY

Supplier Relationship Management began in 1983 when Peter Kraljic, a former McKinsey consultant, told corporate buyers to be more aggressive in supply management.[2] His posture was that buyers should understand their various supply categories' risk and profitability impact upon their organizations, so they could devise the most appropriate supplier strategies. For example, buying paper products for the company doesn't impact profitability, nor does it constitute a supply risk. However, if they had a supply shortage of brushless dc motors, it would impact their daily production output and that of their customers. It would be a significant risk and a huge loss to profitability.

Figure 9–2 shows a purchasing model that identifies four Procurement strategies that can be used with suppliers. This is called the Kraljic Matrix, with an adaptation by Van Weele and Williams and Saine. The model plots the Impact on Financial Results versus the Supply Risks from low to high from Procurement's perspective. It is useful because it allows Procurement to move from analysis to strategy with each supplier.

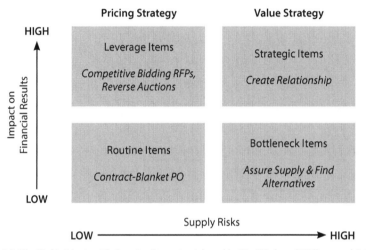

Figure 9-2: The Kraljic Matrix with Sourcing Strategies, Adapted by Van Weele and Williams and Saine.

- Low-Low: In this quadrant, items with a low financial impact and a low supply risk are viewed as Routine items. Products and services in this category are readily available and viewed as a Commodity. The sourcing strategy is to find a supplier at the lowest possible price, consolidate the spend, and issue a blanket purchase order (PO) to keep the transaction costs low. *If you are a supplier in this quadrant, you must be able to compete on price, terms, conditions, and delivery.*

- Low-High: In this quadrant, items with a low impact on financial results and a high supply risk are called Bottleneck items. The sourcing strategy assures a supply by holding inventory. With Bottleneck items, the supplier has leverage because there are usually fewer alternatives for the customer. *The supplier can command a higher price, but they should provide buyers with a volume assurance to allay fears.*

- High-Low: In this quadrant, items with a high impact on the financial results but limited supply risks are called Leverage items. These Leverage items are often viewed as a "buyer's paradise" because there are many suppliers, their offerings are viewed as a commodity, and the switching costs are perceived to be low. Buyers in this category want spend aggregation. As a result, sellers should expect Procurement to use competitive bidding, RFPs, reverse auctions, and tough price negotiations to drive down the price. Sellers in this quadrant *must be able to sell at low cost while still providing value.*

- High-High: In this quadrant, items with a high supply risk and a high financial risk are called Strategic items. The items provided by the supplier are critical for the products' success, so the customer is dependent upon the supplier. The sourcing strategy is to build a solid relationship with the key suppliers and negotiate long-term agreements to ensure a sustainable competitive advantage while conducting contingency planning. *In this quadrant, sellers have the best negotiating position, and they can sell value.*

   Recommended Action: Before negotiating with Procurement, sellers should consider the quadrant in which Procurement has them placed. This knowledge will help sellers understand Procurement's strategy in working with them and their firm. The quadrants on the left are about price, while the quadrants on the right are about value. If you feel your product belongs in a different quadrant, you must provide the business case and get agreement before you begin to negotiate.

WHAT'S ON PROCUREMENT'S DASHBOARD?

As sellers, your performance is under scrutiny. Management has key performance indicators (KPIs) that measure your performance daily, monthly, quarterly, and yearly. The most common KPIs are revenue versus plan, achievement of the assigned product mix, percentage of gross margin, win rates, and expenses versus plan.

Buyers in Procurement have KPIs that measure their performance. By understanding how their performance is measured, you can make it easier to forge a working relationship and achieve mutual goals. It will also allow you to understand their strategies and goals and predict their next move.

While KPIs may vary by organization, consider the list below as a fair representation of how executives measure the contribution of their Procurement teams. If you can positively impact one or more of Procurements KPIs, you can become a respected supplier or trusted partner.

1. **Savings Realized:** This is the hard number that can be quantified as savings resulting from price discounts, change in suppliers, etc. Earnings per share (EPS) impact is also measured, particularly when Procurement is at the C-level and charged with leading enterprise transformation

2. **Spend Under Management:** This is the proportion of the organization's total spend on products (capital and consumables) and purchased services that are under the influence or control of Procurement. The higher the percentage, the lower the chance of "rogue" buying by a department or individual.

3. **Percentage Savings Achieved:** This is often expressed as a percentage of forecast savings. In general, the higher the number, the better Procurement's performance. The reasons for a lower number could be an increase in energy costs, an influx of rush orders, higher-than-expected volumes, or later-than-anticipated start dates from supplier contracts.

4. **Percentage Compliance/Non-Compliance**: This measures the percentage of spend made by rogue buyers who are circumventing the Procurement department. If this number is 50%, it means that 5 out of every 10 dollars (if measured in USA currency) is being spent with unapproved suppliers outside of the agreed-upon contract terms and without adherence to Procurement's policies and procedures.

5. **Internal Client Satisfaction:** This describes how well Procurement responds to providing the product, equipment, or supplies that each

department's stakeholders require when they need it. Think of this as a "delivery to required date." It can be measured as a percentage of on-time shipments that are completed along with stakeholder satisfaction. Remember, Procurement must provide value to their internal stakeholders.

6. **Procurement Cycle Time:** There are two ways to look at this KPI: the average time it takes from submission of the requisition to purchase-order placement, or the time it takes from the beginning of a sourcing process until a contract is signed.

7. **Cost Avoidance:** This is a cost reduction from a lower-than-expected spend that would not have occurred without Procurement's intervention. Examples include contracts that protect price over time, delaying a price increase, or obtaining additional services for free such as staff training and no-charge attendance at a manufacturer's service school.

8. **Supplier Performance:** Procurement always tracks the quality, cost, and delivery of their key suppliers. This often takes the form of a supplier scorecard.

9. **Percentage of Active Suppliers Accounting for 80% of Total Spend:** This KPI measures supplier consolidation and activity from one year to the next. Increased supply usage and new-product introductions can impact this metric.

10. **Procurement Costs:** Procurement costs money in both people and technology. Organizations measure and monitor the cost of providing service within the organization. To cut costs, Procurement often uses a range of strategies such as automation in placing and tracking orders, consolidating suppliers and SKUs, and negotiating longer contracts.

11. **Procurement ROI:** This KPI measures Procurement's cost effectiveness by comparing their cost savings to the department's operating budget.

12. **Percentage of On-Time Delivery** (OTD): This rarely refers to a specific date; it usually refers to a range of dates defined as X days

before (early) and Y days after (late) the due date. A typical OTD window is 5 days early, 0 days late (can be expressed as -5+0). For example, if an item is due September 1, it would be considered on time if it arrives on any day between August 27 and September 1.

Generally, these and other Procurement metrics are defined and tracked on a dashboard like that shown in Figure 9–3.

Examples of Procurement Dashboard Key Performance Indicators

Cost Metrics	Quality Metrics	Service Metrics	Operational Metrics
Savings Realized	Internal Client Satisfaction	Procurement Cycle Time	Percentage of Compliance and Non-Compliance
Spend Under Management	Supplier Performance	Percentage of On-Time Delivery	Percentage of Active Suppliers Accounting for 80% of Total Spend
Percentage Savings Achieved			Procurement ROI
Cost Avoidance			
Procurement Costs			

Figure 9-3 Examples of Procurement Dashboard Key Performance Indicators

Why are these KPIs important? They are critical keys underlying accountability that drives Procurement policies and procedures. When Procurement is successful in helping the organization achieve business goals, it can bring them recognition, bonuses, promotions, additional funding, and self-satisfaction. The lesson: Frenemies help one another achieve their business objectives.

Sellers also need to be prepared to provide KPIs that reflect the very real business benefits when a more-expensive solution is purchased that inures to the benefit of the business but does not appear to be the best choice when measured solely by these Procurement KPIs.

EIGHT STEPS TOP PERFORMERS TAKE TO BUILD COLLABORATION

Do you view Procurement as a threat and necessary evil that must be managed carefully on each deal? Or do you view them as an ally who can help you facilitate the Procurement process? Partner! Don't polarize!

To partner with Procurement, there are eight steps that top performers find helpful.

1. **Understand Procurement's Scorecard Criteria**

   These are for finished goods, packaging, or raw materials suppliers.

   - **Assured Supply**—The supplier can meet the changing demands of the buyer, especially if regulatory requirements change.
   - **Quality**—Items delivered are free of quality issues and meet the specifications of the buyer. This is largely driven by the end user's opinion of the product or service. Everything else—price, quality, etc.—can be great, but if enough users don't like it, Procurement has a problem.
   - **Service**—Supplier is easy to do business with and is constantly seeking ways to improve service.
   - **Cost**—No games. The lowest price is provided initially; all pricing is transparent and competitive, and the supplier agrees to work on cost improvements.
   - **Innovation**—The supplier explores innovative ways to conduct business that reduces costs for the buyer.
   - **Environment and Ethics**—There is alignment between both organizations to be environmentally friendly and to conduct transactions in a business-like manner.

   Recommended Action: Potential suppliers should objectively measure themselves against the incumbent and other potential suppliers to determine where they have a measurable strength and/or weakness to be addressed.

2. **Understand the Types of Procurement Buyers**

   While most large organizations possess savvy and highly talented Procurement professionals, it's always a good practice to assess the sophistication level of each buyer. Figure 9–4 shows four different types of buyers against four different factors and provides a description of each.

	Relationship Buyer	Price Buyer	Competitive Buyer	Value Buyer
Primary Motivation	*Trust:* Buyer wants assurance there is a strong relationship and that their needs will be met.	*Price:* Wants the lowest price—period! Many are prone to use RFPs and other tactics.	*Win:* They mask themselves as value or relationship buyers but are really price buyers.	*Business Impact:* Believes the supplier is helping to drive measurable financial results.
Focus	*Insular:* Relies on the supplier to provide a function they cannot provide internally or be a resource when needed.	*Narrow:* May or may not look at the Total Cost of Ownership (TCO). Differentiation means nothing to them.	*Win: Lose* They must win by driving down price or extracting more value from the supplier.	*Strategic:* Get as much value as they can. Standardization with 1-2 suppliers per product category is customary.
Relationship Type	*Personal:* Values the relationship with the supplier, their industry and product, expertise, support provided, and training offered. Least price sensitive.	*Demanding:* Likes to remind you that he/she has product and service alternatives, so you need to sharpen your pencil to get their business.	*Difficult:* They talk value and relationship, but their actions are all about price.	*Partner/Advisor:* Technology and data driven. Wants hard evidence.
Relationship Level	*Important and Individual:* Strong business relationships exist between one or more people in both organizations.	*Non-Existent:* Business relationships are not viewed as important. Suppliers are treated as a commodity. Procurement rules.	*Gamesmanship:* Uses every negotiation tactic possible to make the seller provide concessions.	*Favorable:* Desires a strong business relationship with key suppliers based upon mutual respect, trust, and value.

Figure 9-4 Four Types of Buyers Against Four Different Factors

Recommended Action: Plan your conversations and negotiations with Procurement, by making notes about what you know or have heard about the Procurement representative. Compare your notes to Figure 9–4, and see which buyer "type" best describes your representative. What motivates his/her type? How does your value proposition align with the Procurement buyer's motivation? What does their focus tell you about how they are likely to negotiate? What should you expect from their "relationship type"? Make your plans accordingly by considering where your product falls in the Kraljic Matrix in Figure 9–2.

3. **Take Steps to Improve Your Company's Standing.**
   There are many reasons why your company may be rated low on a supplier scorecard, including a low fill rate, partial shipments, price variances, price increases, late deliveries, invoice errors, and low Perfect Order results. Lazy, inattentive, seemingly untrustworthy sales people can also create a low supplier score even if everything else is good. Rather than throw the sales representative under the bus, most Procurement pros will opt to change suppliers. It's easier for them to move on.

   Recommended Action: Get your own "house" in order. If you want to collaborate with Procurement, have a candid discussion about their vendor scorecard, and explore steps you can take to be a better supplier. Treat Procurement as having the ultimate vote on "customer experience." Challenge your internal customer support team to help you improve your vendor scorecard in each functional area.

4. **Help Procurement Build a Compelling Business Case for Your Solution.**
   Most sellers hate to build business cases—it's time consuming and complicated. Instead, many just borrow a case built by another representative using different KPIs and different assumptions. "After all, one customer is pretty much like the last." Wrong! Each Procurement team will have different product specifications and KPIs. One may measure a product's Return on Investment, a second may

focus on Total Cost of Ownership, while a third may be concerned with Payback.

Recommended Action: In general, it's a good practice early in the buy-sell process to meet with a Procurement representative to determine their KPIs, preferred formula, and necessary format. Also, when you have completed the business case, schedule a time to meet with your liaison, debrief on your results, and get feedback. If the situation changes, you will be able to adapt before it's too late. In some organizations, such as the example we used at the beginning of this chapter, sales leadership may direct (and the client may allow) sales professionals to go directly to the department/function that will use your product to sell them on your value before going to Procurement. This is a decision that needs to be made by sales leadership in each organization according to how the customer buys.

5. **Craft and Employ Value Messages That Resonate with Procurement.**
Sellers should not succumb to the assumption that Procurement is interested only in price. More likely than not, Procurement will focus on price because it is easily measured and resonates with the executive suite. Every dollar saved by Procurement drops straight through to the bottom line.

Most Procurement buyers focus on the relationship between a product or solution and critical (and measurable) corporate objectives. Value messages that connect the two in a clear, reasonable way are often well received. So, this question arises: "What corporate objectives can be measurably served by your product?" Build messages that clearly articulate the connection. In any sale, approximately 25% of the value provided to a buyer in purchasing a product is attributable to intangibles.

Recommended Action: First, uncover hidden, tangible benefits of your product or solution. A good place to start is to ask your customers to identify soft benefits.

Second, build "personas" for all Procurement personnel and executives. Then craft value messages that connect with their perception of business, financial, and personal benefits. Many successful sales teams rely on "playbooks" to provide a range of value messages that resonate with different buying influences.

6. **Assist Procurement in Understanding the Cost of "Doing Nothing" or "Not Changing."**

Across all industries, there is a tendency for sellers to overlook the power, attractiveness, and internal support that can mobilize around "doing nothing" or "not changing." Doing nothing can cover a broad spectrum of options that range from a decision to not award the contract at this junction, to continue servicing a project or product through internal resources, or retaining a familiar (but flawed) supplier.

Make no mistake, "doing nothing" or "not changing" can be a powerful and safe competitive option. Sellers need to build a compelling case against the status quo with a strong combination of analytics, documentation, and value messages that will appeal to Procurement. (See Chapter 6 on "Selling Against the Status Quo.")

Recommended Action: "Doing nothing" has two attractive benefits to Procurement and internal buyers: it is easy to predict costs and calculate risks. To appeal to Procurement, you must address any suspicion of risk associated with your product or solution that can make "doing nothing" seem unreasonable. Are there implementation issues, training concerns, production challenges, or delivery obstacles that you can address quickly and forcefully? Your challenge is to share with Procurement an "insurance policy" that mitigates risk.

Additionally, you must quantify the costs associated with "no change." Is the buyer trying to circumvent costs in the current year? Are there financial options that you can offer that are unavailable with the status quo? What are the unseen costs of deferring change? This means you must understand and document the full range of costs embedded in the status quo. Help Procurement construct a credible comparison that can be shared and defended in executive-level briefings.

7. **Discover What the Procurement Process Looks Like.**
   Determine the steps, issues, timeline, competitive landscape, signature approval process, etc., so you can work effectively within the guidelines and time requirements specified by Procurement.

   Recommended Action: Learn early who Procurement reports to within the organization and what other projects or tasks are competing for their time and may distract them from evaluating your proposal thoroughly, completely, and fairly.

8. **Keep Your Champion Informed of all Activity and Ask for Assistance as Appropriate.**
   Remember that your Champion has a vested interest in the outcome of your discussions and can speed or expedite approval.

   Recommended Action: Document everything, and share updates with your Champion in a timely fashion. Keep in mind, your Champion may be focused on KPIs that are somewhat different than the Procurement team's.

Sellers should understand that Procurement dramatically improves an organization's bottom line. Every dollar, euro, pound, etc., saved during the negotiation with suppliers goes straight to the bottom line. Procurement also improves working capital, which makes the balance sheet look better. As a result, the Chief Procurement Officer is often the "best friend" of the CEO. He/she is a major player in every institution.

Key Points to Remember:

1. Sellers should understand the differences between how sellers think and how Procurement thinks.
2. Sellers should be able to define the function that Procurement performs.

3. There are 7 common myths about Procurement. Sellers should understand how these myths can misdirect and mislead their sales strategies.

4. Sellers should discover how Procurement has "graded" the selling organization as a supplier.

5. Sellers should discover and craft messages that address Procurement's key performance indicators.

6. Sellers should be able to identify Procurement KPIs that affect their product or service.

7. Sellers should deploy a sales strategy that incorporates the 8 steps to building collaboration with Procurement.

8. Sellers should be able to describe and recognize the different types of buyers. As you prepare for negotiation, use the buyer "types" to help you understand motivation, focus, and relationship preference.

——— YOUR COMMITMENT ———

What is the one thing you will commit to doing differently because of reading this chapter? Please share it here or on a separate sheet of paper.

_____

_____

_____

_____

ADDENDUM 6: PROCUREMENT-READY CHECKLIST

Top performers begin building relationships with Procurement by employing a discovery process. They ask questions to help them understand their customer's desired wins. What are their priorities, interests, requirements, expectations, internal obstacles, and key performance indicators? It's the seller's responsibility, as a partner, to educate, counsel, and guide their customer toward a "win-win" solution. Consider the following checklist to determine if you are "Procurement ready."

Map Procurement's Involvement.

☐ Who from Procurement will be involved in the review and assessment of your proposal?

☐ What is the background and expertise of the Procurement liaison?

☐ Will others in Procurement have a role in the review process?

Understand the Buying Process.

☐ What does the buying process look like, and at what phase are the buyers in their decision process?

☐ Who has ultimate signature authority?

☐ What major obstacles do buyers face when deciding?

Know the Ideal Timeline.

☐ What is the ideal time frame for reaching a buying decision?

☐ What competing projects may delay or derail the decision on your proposal?

☐ What can you do or provide to help Procurement meet their time objective?

Assemble a Compelling Business Case.

☐ Who is assembling a business case that will facilitate Procurement's ability to test or document value?

☐ What are the KPIs that are most important in judging the value of this product proposal?

☐ In what ways has the customer's business model changed in recent months, and what financial measures do they use to make purchasing decisions?

Know Procurement's Deliverable.

☐ What expectations or objectives has senior management established for Procurement?

☐ What dashboard metrics does Procurement use to judge their overall performance and benefit to the organization?

Gauge Openness to Discovery.

☐ How interested and open is Procurement to discovering ways your organization can collaborate with Procurement to help them meet their vital business objectives?

☐ Would they be open to an "executive roundtable" to discuss options that would serve their financial interest?

Know Your Competitive Landscape.

☐ What are their options and alternatives to your proposal?

☐ How feasible is it for your customer to "do nothing"?

☐ What is the cost and risk to your customer of "doing nothing"?

☐ Who is your strongest competitor, and what advantage do they provide?

Provide Differentiation.

☐ How can you articulate a compelling advantage that connects with their KPIs, supports their business model, and differentiates your company from a strong competitor?

☐ What references, case studies, or referrals can you provide that Procurement would find helpful?

Chapter 10

The Price Is Never Right

Managing Price-Discount Demands

"Over time, if we aren't tracking pricing and margins across all our deals, we may find we've gotten into very bad discounting practices."

Dave Brock—author of *Sales Manager's Survival Guide*

Whoever you are, whatever you sell, price can become a vexing issue between yourself and your customers. Let's explore the many challenges, implications, and best practices for handling price issues in general and demands for a price discount in particular. Consider the story of the seller with beans in his ears.

Story: The Seller with Beans in His Ears

Several years ago, we were meeting with a regional sales vice president for a company that sells foodservice systems to government facilities and hospitals. We were in a planning session when the telephone in the room rang. The SVP answered, listened for a moment, and then said, "I'm going to put one of my sales representatives on the speakerphone. I'd like to get your thoughts." We listened as the SVP said, "Why don't you start at the beginning. I've got two consultants here, and, between the four of us, we ought to be able to find a solution." The sales representative explained that he had submitted a strong proposal for an $8M opportunity. He was well positioned with the executive buyer and expected a quick "Yes" to close the deal. That morning, he received a call that didn't go as he anticipated. The sales representative explained, "My customer wants a 'sweeter' deal. He says there's a big 'financial disconnect.' I don't need to remind you that we worked hard to get him the best deal possible, and we don't have room to squeeze out more money. We could be upside down in this thing."

When the SVP hung up the phone, he looked puzzled and said, "There is something strange here. I met with this customer several weeks ago and walked him through all aspects of the deal. I think I need to step away to make a phone call and talk to the customer and hear his side firsthand."

When the SVP returned, he had a big smile on his face. "I knew it! I knew it!" He explained that the prospective customer had made a mistake when estimating the costs of the overall project. His budget office caught the mistake and was threatening to hold up the deal—not because of the sales representative's proposal but because the buying organization miscalculated the cost. During his phone call with the client, the SVP put a quick solution on the table. He proposed to reduce the cost of products and services in year one and increase the costs in years 2 through 5 of the five-year contract. This helped the customer and the budget office sign off on the deal.

The sales representative didn't hear what his prospect was really saying. He heard only the panic and quickly concluded that the deal was falling apart. Instead, the SVP listened, identified the problem, and outlined a solution. He lowered the price during the first year and increased the price over the remaining years of the contract.

> **Seller's Challenge:** *Optimize Revenue and Profit by Managing Price Demands that Threaten to Disrupt or Undermine the Sale*
>
> Almost every buyer wants to negotiate a lower price. Buyers often demand that a seller discount the price of products or services. This may be in direct conflict with the selling organization's profitability targets or their incentive-compensation program that's meant to increase or maintain gross margins. Buyer demands often take the form of divisive tactics that can plague or kill a sales opportunity. The challenge for sellers is to discover the needs of the buyer's organization, identify options, and prepare to negotiate an outcome that is beneficial for both the buyer and seller.

The purpose of this chapter is to prepare sellers to negotiate pricing demands effectively. Sellers will learn how to understand the buyer's mindset about price, anticipate price challenges, and choose wise counter-moves that protect both profit and commission.

WHY THE PRICE OBSESSION?

Let's begin with a quick look at the buyer's mindset. Why are some buyers fixated on price? What steps can you take to prepare yourself for price-driven bargaining?

Consider the following five factors for a buyer's price obsession:

1. **Competitors have developed a pricing strategy that encourages price discounting**. This strategy allows competitors the flexibility to propose a price and then discount it when faced with a price demand. With each passing year, buyers become convinced that this is how all sellers operate.

2. **Price may be the only value that differentiates products, services, and solutions.** In other words, sellers fail to demonstrate compelling, quantifiable value beyond price. Let's face it: price is easily quantified, and everyone knows what it means.

3. **Buyers believe that "competition" will guarantee a reduced price**. In an RFP process, buyers expect that one or more bids will undercut their current price. In truth, products are more and more

sophisticated, and prices reflect the increased costs of production and innovation.

4. **Sellers often misread a buyer's concern as a price concern**. Let's take an example. Suppose a customer says, "We can't afford your proposal." Is that a price concern? It may be a price concern or an outburst resulting from frustration with the negotiation process. The seller's challenge is to ask questions that uncover the reasons for the outburst.

5. **Some buyers view price demands as a responsible business practice.** Consequently, these buyers request price reductions on everything from product price to shipping, training, and repair. Often, they measure their own performance in dollars saved from the original price.

THREE PATHWAYS TO MANAGING PRICE-DISCOUNT DEMANDS

In every price-driven negotiation, there are three pathways open to the seller. No path is right or wrong. All have benefits and risks—all require preparation and skill. A seller faces three options when challenged with a demand for a price discount:

- Seller can "hold" to the original price
- Seller can concede to the price discount requested
- Seller can offer provisions that satisfy the buyer's interests without conceding the full amount of the price discount requested.

Let's look at these three options and the essential steps to prepare for them.

Managing Price-Discount Demands, Option #1: Seller Holds to Original Price

This can be a treacherous path to follow unless you plan it well in advance. Without preparation, a "hold the price" response can make sellers appear inflexible or stubborn, and unwilling to negotiate. It may not kill the negotiation, but it could make it very difficult. If buyers perceive inflexibility, they have a habit of retaliating with their own stubborn responses on other issues. "Paybacks" can make for tough negotiations.

"Without preparation, a 'hold the price' response can make sellers appear inflexible or stubborn, and unwilling to negotiate. It may not kill the negotiation, but it could make it very difficult."

How can you prepare in advance to make "hold the price" responses more acceptable to the buyer? Early in the sales process, explain to the buyer that your initial proposal will be the best financial deal you can offer. As the buy-sell process evolves, reiterate your plan, but explain that as your partnership grows, you both may discover additional cost-saving measures like a sole supplier contract and discounts resulting from an extended contract.

During the sales process, you should determine who initiated the "ask" for a price discount. Is it the buyer or someone else in the organization? What's their rationale for a price discount? For example you might ask, "We've talked about price on several occasions. What's motivating your request for a lower price?"

When you've prepared well and kept your buyer aware of pricing restrictions, you spare the buyer from experiencing "sticker shock." You also make them aware of future possibilities for price restructuring.

For a complete summary of the "Hold the Price" approach with essential steps to success, the risks, and the benefits, see Figure 10–1.

"Sellers should forewarn the buyer of a fixed price early in the buying process."

Seller's Response to Price Discount Request	• Seller holds to the original price and refuses the request.
Overview of the Pricing Approach	• In some industries, the buyer expects the first bid or quoted price to be the best offer. • Some state governments and federal agencies stipulate that the seller provide a "best offer" in their initial proposal. • When a buyer is purchasing a rare product with limited availability or distribution, the initial cost may reflect limited supply.
Steps Essential to Success	• Seller should develop a strong pricing rationale that explains why the seller is unable to decrease the price. For example, the product may be new and perform the function of two products. • Seller should craft a compelling value proposition that resonates with the buyer. • Seller should forewarn the buyer of a fixed price early in the buying process. • Seller should quantify the financial and non-financial benefits of the product or service in a head-to-head comparison with the primary competitor. • Seller should identify any conditions that would lower the overall cost to the buyer, such as larger orders, buying additional products, or extending the length of the contract. • Seller should focus the discussion and negotiation on Payback or Total Cost of Ownership instead of price.
Risks	• The seller may appear inflexible or unresponsive.
Benefits	• Fixed pricing optimizes revenue and profit for the seller. • Seller's product may be perceived as a value purchase instead of a commodity.

Figure 10-1 Seller Holds Price to the Original Offer

Managing Price-Discount Demands, Option #2: Seller Concedes to Discount

In today's global business environment, deals can range from the thousands of dollars to millions. As a common business practice, buyers request options, favorable payment terms, and discounts. Be careful what you concede.

 "As a common business practice, buyers request options, favorable payment terms, and discounts. Be careful what you concede."

Many sellers have predetermined limits for discounting their products and services. In other words, a seller may have a 5 or 10% leeway to modify an initial offer. That doesn't mean it's necessary or advisable to provide the full discount. In fact, the seller should not use their leeway unless there is overwhelming evidence that they will lose the deal without some adjustment in price. Sellers can misuse their discount privileges. We hear stories about sellers who make the following mistakes and cost their companies revenue and profit—while taking money out of their own pockets by compromising their commissions.

Sellers misuse discount privileges when they tell their buyers:

- *"If you think our price is high, let me know because I can make an adjustment."*
- *"If you need a 5% discount, I can make that happen."*
- *"Our pricing is just a starting point."*
- *"Tell me where I need to be."*

Consider what this does to the buyer's expectation in future transactions. The expectation will be for a minimum 5% discount—possibly much greater. Unwise concessions can quickly erode profit and change a "career making" deal into a "career breaking" deal.

 Unwise concessions can quickly erode profit and change a "career making" deal into a "career breaking" deal.

For a summary of the essential steps to success, the risks, and the benefits of an effective concession to a price demand, see Figure 10–2.

Many sellers have predetermined limits for discounting their products and services. In other words, a seller may have a 5 or 10% leeway for adjusting their proposed price. Oftentimes, this is available in tiers. One of our clients uses the following guidelines:

- The sales representative should always quote list price and attempt to hold it.
- The sales representative can authorize up to a 5% discount for a "written order or verbal PO" today. They must provide their Region Sales Manager with a written justification for the discount.

- The sales representative can ask their Region Sales Manager to approve up to a 10% discount. The order size must be "A" amount or larger (cases, pallets, currency etc.) and it must be placed by "B" date.
- Discount requests over 10% must be submitted to and approved by the Region Sales Manager and VP Sales. The order size must be "X" amount or larger (cases, pallets, currency etc.) and it must be placed by "Y" date.

Seller's Response to Price Discount Request	• Seller concedes the discount and amends the product price per the seller's discount demand or they reach a mutually acceptable compromise.
Overview of the Pricing Approach	• Most sellers' organizations anticipate the demand for a price discount and build in leeway for a discount as part of their pricing strategy. A variety of discount opportunities may come into play, such as discounts for volume or for the purchase of additional products in the portfolio.
Steps Essential to Success	• Make sure the price concession is the only remaining obstacle to concluding the deal. • Make the concession difficult and hard-fought. Otherwise the buyer may think that they should have struck a better deal. • Make sure the buyer understands that the discount is a one-time exception and not applicable to other products or services.
Risks	• The seller sets a future expectation for price discounts on the same product. For example, by conceding to a request for a 5% discount, the seller sets an expectation that, in future negotiations, the seller will provide a 5% discount, at a minimum. • The seller compromises profit and revenue performance with a discounted price.
Benefits	• Sellers should ask themselves, "What have I bought with my willingness to concede to the buyer's demand?" "Did I ask for a benefit in return such as access to other buyers in the organization for other products?" Make sure you get something from giving something.

Figure 10-2 Seller Concedes to Price-Discount Demand

Managing Price-Discount Demands, Option #3:

Seller Uses Trades and Bundles to Minimize Price Concessions

By building options in anticipation of a price-discount demand—a trading plan—the seller may avoid being trapped into a priced-driven negotiation that compromises revenue and profit. A trading plan is a seller's plan for reaching a "win-win" settlement through give-and-take. It is sometimes referred to as a "concession strategy."

> *"A trading plan is a seller's plan for reaching a win-win settlement through give-and-take. It is sometimes referred to as a 'concession strategy.'"*

A trading plan requires preparation and planning. Top performers begin by listing all the interests, issues, or points of potential conflict that may arise. It will likely include several financial and non-financial issues as well as terms and conditions. The trading plan should include all the high-priority interests that are important for both parties and must include any potential points of disagreement that could obstruct the negotiation or derail discussions. Interests are the essential components of an agreement. They describe the needs, wants, desires, and motivators of each party. Interests are the driving force behind negotiation.

Often professional negotiators will meet with their counterparts before the formal negotiating session to identify interests and concerns. Others may use brainstorming to develop an agenda of issues and concerns.

Experienced negotiators construct possible "positions." In collaborative negotiations, a position is a thoughtfully conceived option designed to satisfy both parties' interests on a given issue or point of contention. In this regard, negotiators are problem solvers who are exploring options that may satisfy the interests of both parties.

Many inexperienced negotiators find themselves surprised by their counterpart's requests and react by conceding a point of contention without testing what they can get in return. In other words, they "give away" something to comply with the buyer's demand.

This is where strategy plays an important role. Should I begin with a weak position and enhance my offer over two or three subsequent positions? Should I concede the point, or should I ask for something of similar value in return?

When you prepare thoroughly, you reduce surprises and avoid unnecessary "giveaways." Your trading plan can be derived from your answer to a single question: "*What combination of options is most likely to satisfy the underlying interests of both parties on each critical issue?*"

Consider the trading-plan benefits, risks, and steps essential to success as outlined in Figure 10–3.

Seller's Response to Buyer's Request	• Seller employs trades and bundles to create a win-win negotiation that advances the interests of both parties.
Overview of Price Response	• At times sellers must take a step back from price-driven negotiations, grasp all the conditions, provisions, terms, and costs at stake, and recognize that the goal is to satisfy each party's primary interests. What factors drive those interests? What financial and non-financial options can unify the two parties?
Steps Essential to Success	• Seller should hold preliminary discussions that focus on the discovery of underlying interests and concerns. • Seller prepares a compelling value proposition that allows a rich discussion of benefits beyond price. • Seller prepares bundles and packages of financial and non-financial options that are designed to satisfy a buyer's interests.
Risks	• Seller depends on the buyer's willingness to disclose their interests and work collaboratively, so the seller can create trades and bundles. • The process may not work well with competitive buyers or buyers who see the product as a commodity.
Benefits	• This process provides significant flexibility and addresses a range of interests. • This format can promote disclosure and trust. • This approach helps sellers preserve revenue and profit.

Figure 10-3 Seller Uses Trades and Bundles to Satisfy Buyer Interests

As you plan your trades and bundles, review the options in "Addendum 7: Options for Trades and Bundles." It provides ideas for adding non-financial value to your trade, and it shows you how to add financial horsepower without eroding the price.

Conceding to Price Demands: What Are the Downsides?

What are the three challenges of discounting?

1. It decreases profitability and increases the number of deals you must win to achieve your revenue goal.

2. It sends the wrong signal to buyers. Price discounts tell buyers that pricing is flexible and that you don't really believe in the value you create. It sets a precedent, suggesting the current product and all other products can be discounted.

3. It often provides discounts to the wrong company or for the wrong reasons.

Most sales representatives don't fully understand the effects of price discounts on gross margins or unit sales because they have never been taught to think financially. Sellers are usually more concerned with concluding the deal than protecting margins.

Every time a seller discounts a product or service, he/she or the organization must increase their unit volume to make up the price difference. Unless they are paid on gross margin, sellers have no concept of the monetary effects of price discounting. Figure 10–4 illustrates how price discounting affects the unit sales required to maintain the same gross margin.

For example, if everyone in the sales organization discounted their sales 10% at a 50% gross margin, it would necessitate a 25% increase in unit sales to make the same revenue goal and profit margin.

Figure 10–4 also shows why discount guidelines should be in writing and show sales representatives and managers how much of a discount they can offer before they need to obtain further approval from senior leadership. Guidelines also demonstrate the need for an organization to achieve revenue numbers at the stipulated gross margin to meet profit goals.

Although Figure 10–4 shows price concessions in 5% increments, consider increments of 1.5% or 3%—when price concessions are essential for closing a deal.

Gross Margin Before the Price Decrease	Price Discounts			
	-5%	-10%	-15%	-20%
	Unit Sales Must Increase by the Following to Maintain the Same Gross Margin Dollars!			
60% Gross Margin	+9%	+20%	+33%	+50%
55% Gross Margin	+10%	+22%	+37.5%	+57%
50% Gross Margin	+11%	+25%	+43%	+67%
45% Gross Margin	+13%	+29%	+50%	+80%
40% Gross Margin	+14%	+33%	+60%	+100%
35% Gross Margin	+17%	+40%	+75%	+133%
30% Gross Margin	+20%	+50%	+100%	+200%

Figure 10-4 Effects of Price Discounts on Gross Margins and Unit Sales

HOW TOP PERFORMERS PREPARE FOR PRICE-DRIVEN NEGOTIATIONS

A webcast[1] sponsored by Harvard University's Program on Negotiation made an excellent argument for price-discount preparation. The speaker explained that everything in a bargaining session can be anticipated. His point was that if you prepare adequately, you'll be ready for any eventuality. Let's look at how sellers need to research, anticipate, and plan.

Bargaining preparation can be divided into three actions:

1. Formulate a "seller's profile" that covers all price-related terms and conditions to be negotiated (i.e., What are *your* interests?)
2. Create a "buyer's profile" that covers all price-related terms and conditions to be negotiated (i.e., What's *your customer's* interests?)
3. Anticipate the buyer's tactics, and plan your counter-moves (What are your potential concessions, and where will you hold firm?)

1. Formulate a Seller's Profile. As the seller, there are several questions you must ask and answer for yourself on each cost item to be negotiated. Remember that some deals embrace more than one product or may include conditions that have an associated price. For example, in one sale there may be a software license that constitutes the "big ticket" item in the deal. But there may be smaller-ticket items that could become obstacles as well, such as costs to customize modules in the software, training costs to bring the customer's staff up to speed, or on-site monitoring of performance during the implementation period. For each of these cost items, the seller should consider the following questions.

- *"What is my price target?"* The "target" is the best and most appropriate price that the seller can expect from the bargaining process. For many sellers, the "target" price is the price specified in their proposal. However, some selling organizations have a pricing structure that anticipates discounting prices to ensure the buyer feels like they have received a good deal.
- *"What is my 'walk away' price?"* This may be the lowest price authorized (by the selling organization) for the product or service, or it could be the point at which the deal no longer makes financial or business sense for the seller.
- *"How have I demonstrated value and differentiated my product or solution from competitive options?"* If you haven't built a compelling value proposition that differentiates your product, expect your customer to default to price considerations.
- *"Are there payment conditions or financing options that I should discuss with my customer if pricing concerns arise?"*
- *"What is my competitive position? Is my proposal the only option? Am I competing with a current supplier? Am I renewing an existing contract?"*
- *"How have we handled pricing issues with this customer in the past?"* Prior pricing practices may have set an expectation for discounts.
- *"Have I created a compelling business case? Have I positioned the product price in the context of business metrics such as ROI, Payback, and Total Cost of Ownership?"*

2. Create a Buyer's Profile. Great negotiators build a negotiating profile of the buyer, buying committee, or group—early in the sales process.

Reflect on past conversations with the buyer and stakeholders. What matters most to each stakeholder? Consider these questions when creating a "buyer's profile."

- *"What is my best estimate of the buyer's target price?"* What do they want from this purchase?
- *"What is my best estimate of the buyer's 'walk away' point?"* The "walk away" point in price negotiations is the price above which the buyer walks away from the negotiation and focuses on a less-expensive option. Everyone has some flexibility in pricing. How much flexibility have they shown in past negotiations?
- *"What value claims have resonated with my buyer?"* If your value message was well received, it should increase buyer flexibility.
- *"What—aside from price—differentiates my solution from a present supplier or other competitors?"* What's my unique strength and what need does it address?
- *"What is the buyer's view of my competitive position?"* If you are in the lead position, you may not want to offer the same deal you would offer if you were in the middle of the pack.
- *"What pricing experience or history may be driving this buyer's expectations and tactics?"* For some buyers, pushing discounts is "just business." If they can get something, that great. If they can't, then they've tried their best.
- *"What business benefits or underlying needs are driving this purchase?"* The greater the need, the more the buyer will focus on the product or solution that addresses that need.
- *"Are there other stakeholders in the buying organization that might add perspective on pricing?"*
- *"In the case of a contract renewal where the buyer is looking for operating-cost reductions with the new deal, what is the savings threshold I need to meet or surpass for my customer to make a switch? Will they convert to another vendor for 5% savings? 10% savings? 15%?"* Hand in hand with this consideration is the cost of change and perceived risk of change.

Often the cost of retraining, retooling, and reworking processes and protocols, etc., may dictate that savings need to be more than 15% for the change to make financial sense for the organization. Simply put, in the buyer's profile, what is the financial threshold for change?

3. Anticipate Buyer Tactics and Plan Counter-Moves. There are many ways buyers leverage their positions to drive down the pricing of a supplier. Let's consider a couple of the most common tactics and counter-moves that sellers should anticipate. These "competitive" tactics are meant to manipulate the seller by altering their perception of available options.

- **Extreme Price Demands.** One of the most common tactics used by buyers is an extreme price demand. Sometimes the demand can be a simple requirement: "We must get our costs under control, and we're expecting our suppliers to help us out. Let me be more specific—we're expecting a 10% price reduction."

  Recommended Action: The best approach in managing this type of tactic is to explore the buyer's rationale. Ask the buyer, "Help me understand your thinking on a price discount." "Our pricing has been consistent throughout the industry. Is there an example or situation that has influenced your thinking?" Reassure the buyer that you are committed to getting them the best overall deal. "You know our history together and know that we will always provide you the best possible price based upon the circumstances."

- **Ultimatums and Threats.** We've all experienced ultimatums and threats in our business and personal lives. The purpose of an ultimatum or threat is simple: strike fear into one's counterpart and establish a demand as the only option for reaching a settlement. An ultimatum is a "bridge burning" tactic. It destroys rapport and any foundation for collaboration. It's a form of bullying that often surfaces late in a negotiation session due to frustration.

Recommended Action: Many threats are not ultimatums; they are an expression of disappointment and frustration. The buyer wants progress on restructuring the price. The seller should probe for the buyer's perception of "a lower price." Is it 1% lower, 3%, or something else? If the buyer has not already made a formal offer, the seller can encourage the buyer to make one.

HOW TOP PERFORMERS MANAGE FOUR "PRICE CONVERSATIONS"

Savvy sellers do more than prepare for price negotiations; they are skilled at engaging buyers in "price conversations" throughout the buying process. Early in the buying process, sellers want to verify that the buyer has adequate financial resources for the purchase. Skilled sellers guide buyer price expectations. No one wants "sticker shock" to derail negotiations as the deal moves toward closure.

As the buying process continues, sellers help buyers understand and appreciate the value of their product or solution and the benefit to the overall buying organization. Sellers also explore the buyer's expectations for price, their flexibility, and their appreciation for non-financial benefits. Skilled negotiators also formalize trades and offer non-financial deals that minimize price concessions.

There are four types of price conversations that can serve to bring a buyer and seller closer together. In complex B2B deals, these conversations may occur at different points in time. In simpler sales with shorter buy-sell cycles, conversations may be blended. Consider your mastery of four price-driven conversations.

1. **The Expectation Conversation.** *The seller attempts to establish common "points of reference" or expectations on price by offering* an "anchor" and asking probing questions. An anchor is the initial number or price proposed in a negotiation. Psychologists have noted that anchors draw disproportionate attention and focus in the

negotiation process (called "anchoring bias"). *Anchors set expectations and focus conversations.*

In addition to anchors, there are many ways that a seller can guide a buyer's price expectations. For example, a seller can combine an anchor with an explanation of how the price was formulated or share what other buyers have paid and why.

During the "expectation conversation," the seller may attempt to uncover the buyer's target and walk-away price. A seller may ask, "Do you have adequate financial resources for a project that is likely to cost upward of $35,000?" This sets an expectation in the buyer's mind that the price will be close to $35,000. Effective questions can set "points of reference" in framing the buyer's expectations.

2. **The Interests and Options Conversation.** *The seller explores interests (or needs) the buyer and the buying organization are attempting to address through the purchase or negotiation.* However, interests often change during the negotiation process.

   Skilled negotiators explore ways to expand the deal (often called "expand the pie") and broaden the scope of the partnership with a continuing focus on addressing the buyer's underlying interests. For example, a seller might ask, "What interests motivate this purchase?" Or, "What are you hoping to accomplish from this business deal?"

   The seller also looks for signs of flexibility that may open the discussion to non-financial options that minimize price concessions. The seller is thinking, "If I can identify the buyer's interests, I will be closer to understanding what matters most to my counterpart."

3. **The Value & Currency Conversation.** *In this conversation, the seller shares the unique benefits of the seller's product or solution while translating what appears to be price issues into other forms of value (currency) such as time, people, risk abatement, and opportunity.* Skilled negotiators prompt the buyer to focus on unresolved issues and opportunities as well as expose risks that may surface without the purchase of their product.

Research from many quarters has demonstrated that "fear" from an unaddressed "risk" is a far greater motivator to buy than the opportunity to achieve a "gain." For example, "If you don't order and replace this equipment now, you risk losing $10,000 per work hour for weeks until we can get you a new unit." This is far more powerful than saying "Buying our new equipment today will give you an ROI in 12 months."

Additionally, the seller will want to uncover other price options that are available to the buyer. Is the seller well positioned when competitive options (including the status quo) are considered? If both parties can agree on a combination of price and non-financial provisions, will this deal close?

4. **The Binding Agreement Conversation.** This conversation is often what we refer to as "closing the deal" or "negotiating a close." *When considering the agreement in its totality, does the deal adequately serve the interests and underlying needs of both parties?* Is there a solid business case for closing the deal? Can the deal withstand internal review by the buying organization?

What happens when sellers don't engage the buyer in these price conversations?

- The buyer stays with the status quo.
- The buyer and seller may reach a price impasse because the seller's walk-away price is higher than the buyer's walk-away price.
- The seller must concede to a low price in order to close the deal, forfeiting revenue and profit.
- The seller opens the door to a low-price competitor and loses the sale.

GUERRILLA TACTICS FOR PRICE NEGOTIATIONS

Not all "playing fields" are equal or fair. Occasionally sellers may be faced with buying processes that limit unfairly a seller's ability to express the full range of value to the buying organization. When the requirements of the buying process are overly restrictive, it may be useful to turn to tactics that are unconventional or even disruptive.

The purpose of guerrilla and disruptive tactics is several-fold:

- To contest the "process as usual" approach deployed by the buyer
- To reposition your solution in a new light with buyers and stakeholders
- To pique the buyer's interest and curiosity
- To create new standards for judging value

When disruptive tactics are required, you may wish to consider one or more of the following three approaches:

1. **Submit multiple purchase options.** You may wish to take the "good, better, best" approach to give the buyer a full range or options from which to choose. There are two reasons for offering multiple options. First, it focuses the buyer's attention on your purchase options instead of a competitor's offer. Second, it allows you to show the buyer that, when they pay more, they get important benefits in return. Many top performers have found success in offering a "good, better, best" trio of purchase options.

2. **Offer future benefits.** For example, while the buyer may not be eligible at present for a volume discount, you can set expectations based upon the likely future demand for your product by the buying organization. This approach may involve price discounts for volume, benefits from a loyalty program, planned product improvements, and expanded customer services.

3. **Cross-sell products.** Cross-selling can be an effective way to "expand the pie." Savvy sellers discover additional products or services that their organization can provide to the buying organization and that others cannot. Expand the scope of your proposal to offer products and services of value that have not been requested by the buyer. When the playing field favors another supplier, cross-selling may

be an effective way to differentiate your company and products without competing on price alone.

TOP PERFORMERS SHARE "WHAT WORKS"

Over the last several years, we have had the opportunity to work with companies servicing a variety of industries. While our discussions with sales managers and executives have spanned a broad range of topics, one of the most frequently asked questions is: "What guidance can you give our frontline sales representatives when faced with demands for price discounts or concessions?"

There is no shortage of articles addressing how to handle price demands, but we seldom read what frontline representatives identify as best practices. So, we began collecting "messages from the field." In other words, we began asking top-performing sellers to identify "what works" and "what doesn't work" for them when addressing demands for price discounts. Here is what they have said.

1. Prepare before beginning the negotiation. A lack of preparation can cost you money and credibility.
2. Track pricing and gross margins across all deals. Make sure you're not giving discounts for the wrong reasons or to the wrong company.
3. Determine your interests and those of the buyers. Instead of thinking of the people you will negotiate with as adversaries, think of them as partners in the deal.
4. Analyze the options that each side has available. Write them down along with their "pros and cons."
5. Determine your counterpart's walk-away price and your own.
6. Remember to stay calm, cool, and collected. Keep the emotional advantage. Focus on interests and issues, not personalities or words. Even in the most hostile situations, you should take the role of the "adult in the room."

7. Document everything in writing immediately following the meeting, and send it to the other party. Don't allow misperceptions or misinterpretations.

8. Build rapport with the other party. It will help you uncover their needs, show genuine interest in crafting a win-win strategy, and help you both develop more creative options to meet your needs.

9. Listen—then ask good, insightful questions. Good negotiators are detectives. They ask good questions and listen.

10. Do your homework. Gather as much information as you can about your buyers prior to the negotiation. How is their effectiveness measured? What pressures do they bear? To whom do they report? What options do they have? The more information you have, the more effective your negotiating efforts will be.

11. Be prepared to walk away. Not all deals are acceptable financial deals for you and your company. Be prepared to walk away from bad business. Know your walk-away price and respect your limits.

12. Think creatively. Look for ways to expand the deal, not to divide it up equally. Consider "expanding the pie" rather than "dividing the pie."

13. Keep your business case close at hand for easy reference.

14. Be the record and scorecard keeper; keep accurate notes about concessions, changes, and points of agreement.

15. Seek to understand the consequences of not coming to an agreement for both the buyer and the seller. What interests of the buyer are NOT served if an agreement on price can't be reached? Put these consequences on the table during your negotiation.

Today, buyers are more skilled and prepared than in the past. They are more aware of pricing strategies throughout their industry, more knowledgeable of side-by-side product comparisons, and more willing to change suppliers to meet corporate financial benchmarks.

One lesson is vital to winning and surviving price-driven negotiations. Don't live with the buyer's number. Do your own research on what is fair and equitable. Almost every number you hear from a buyer is exaggerated, with the intent to drive you to a price concession. This is what buyers know how to do best. Your job is to change the "currency" of the conversation and focus on the unique value that your product or solution provides the buying organization.

Suppose a buyer indicates she must have a 5% discount on your proposed product price. Does this mean she won't accept a 4.7% discount or a 4.5% reduction? Don't match the buyer's demand with a full price concession. Build a package of options that are attractive without compromising your revenue and profit.

As you prepare a response to price-discount demands, consider the Checklist in Addendums 7 and 8 of this chapter.

Key Points to Remember

1. Sellers should prepare for price-driven bargaining by creating a buyer's profile and a seller's profile.
2. Sellers should anticipate buyer tactics and plan counter-moves.
3. The buyer's walk-away point in a price negotiation is the price at which the buyer turns away from the negotiation to focus on a less-expensive option.
4. The two most common buyer tactics are extreme price demands and ultimatums and threats.
5. Top performers consistently track price discounts and gross margins across all deals.
6. Highly skilled sellers understand how to engage buyers in "price conversations" through the course of the buying process.
7. An initial price anchor can help align a buyer's price expectation with your target price.
8. Discover ways to satisfy a buyer's underlying interests without relying on price concessions.
9. Think creatively, and look for ways to "expand the pie" and enlarge the scope of the partnership.
10. Price is not the only currency that can benefit buyers; think in terms of time, people, risk abatement, and opportunity.

11. Be prepared to walk away if what the buyer is willing to pay is below your walk-away price.

12. When you find yourself on the losing side of a price-driven competition, you may wish to consider disruptive tactics like submitting multiple offers, providing future benefits or incentives, or cross-selling to differentiate benefits beyond price.

YOUR COMMITMENT

What is the one thing you will commit to doing differently because of reading this chapter? Please share it here or on a separate sheet of paper.

_____

_____

_____

_____

ADDENDUM 7: CHECK LIST FOR HANDLING DISCOUNT DEMANDS

This checklist will help sellers and selling teams prepare for complex discount negotiations.

Ready or Not Ready	Recommended Action	Reason
	Probe the buyer's needs and interests; prepare questions.	For the negotiation to be collaborative, you will need to discover all the issues that drive discounting demands, so you can appraise your options realistically. You also need to understand the consequences for your customer if a deal is not reached.
	Create an agenda that can be reviewed with your counterpart. Plan financial and price discussions later in the session.	An agenda gives both parties a comfort level that priority issues will be discussed in time. You may need discussion time to share your value proposition and explain how your product/service can be differentiated from the competition.
	Develop a comprehensive profile of your counterpart. Identify priorities and known tactics. What KPIs will connect with their interests? Are they authorized to make a final decision?	Know your counterpart's expertise and technical background.
	Prepare a quick story or anecdote about a current client that illustrates the value of your solution for them. Organize documentation to support your value claims.	Stories and anecdotes create an emotional connection that resonates with buyers. Documentation strengthens the connection between your value claims and your client's needs.
	Never close quickly. Make the buyer work for closure. Take your time, and cover all issues, terms, and conditions. Make sure that all buyer concerns are addressed.	Buyers will appreciate your decision to be thorough instead of desperate. Buyers are more likely to regret a decision if the process was incomplete.
	Prepare to defuse threats and ultimatums. If you suspect your counterpart is likely to play "hardball" or has a reputation for threats, then prepare for the worst.	The purpose of a threat is to panic the seller. The buyer wants the seller to fear losing the sale if the seller doesn't concede quickly. Take a breath. Relax. Reassure the buyer that you want to get them an acceptable price. Then pose questions to escape their trap.

Ready or Not Ready	Recommended Action	Reason
	Prepare for extreme anchors and lowball offers.	Often a buyer will suggest an extremely low price to divert discussion away from the seller's proposed price. Once they refocus you on their lower price, the buyer can make a small concession.
	Know your walk-away point. Be prepared to explain your why and what this means for your proposal.	Every negotiator must recognize that discussions can cease to be productive. Know when that could happen and how to react.
	Create a list of trades that can help you avoid price discounts. Instead, offer non-financial options that address your customer's interests.	You can divert the conversation from a focus on price discounts if you plan ahead with trades and "bundles."

ADDENDUM 8: POSSIBLE OPTIONS FOR TRADES & BUNDLES

When you build your trading plan, consider these monetary and non-monetary options.

Agreement Types

- Consumables agreement
- Reagent agreement
- Cost per procedure or usage
- Services agreement
- Pay per placement of a full-time equivalent
- Percent from funds collected
- Risk Sharing

Price

- Quantity pricing, i.e., pricing tiers
- Rebates
- Trade-in allowance
- Pricing confidentiality
- Guaranteed pricing for "x" years
- Price-escalation clause
- Line-item pricing
- Category-capitated pricing
- Contract-capitated pricing

Payment Terms

- Length
- Discounts for early pay, specials or incentives, and quantity (initial orders and reorders)
- Cancellation fees

Payment Options

- Purchase
- Rental
- Rent-to own
- Lease

Warranty

- Length
- Price
- Coverage
- Effective date
- Exclusions

Performance Metrics

- Speed of product delivery: from stock, made to order, and emergency delivery
- Guaranteed lead times
- Volume for number of units used or purchased within a time frame, bulk buy, or frequency
- Back orders and product availability
- Shipment frequency
- Product returns
- Purchase commitments—minimum quantities to be ordered
- Consignment inventory
- Inventory management
- Guaranteed uptime

Service Level

- After-sales support—priority or scheduled routine maintenance
- Product or service training for their personnel
- Vendor-service penalties
- Response time for repairs
- After-hours support
- Upgrades
- Customized reports
- Loaner equipment
- Back-up equipment
- Cost-reduction ideas
- Part pricing
- Service terms
- Service plans
- On-site training

Contract Length/Type

- Multi-year agreement
- Renewal rates—automatic renewal or cancellation clauses

Relationship Factors

- Product endorsements
- Access to pilot new products
- Supplier status—exclusive vendor or prime vendor
- Number of suppliers on contract
- Consulting

Contract Terms

- Chargebacks
- Late shipments

Rebates/Allowances

- Total purchases
- Advertising
- Photography
- Defective product

Chargebacks

- Contract violations: early or late shipments, packaging errors, etc.
- Excessive returns
- Defective product
- Excessive markdowns
- Invoice inaccuracies

These are examples only and not meant to be an exhaustive list.

Notes and References

CHAPTER 1: SELLING TO MULTIPLE BUYERS: DISCOVERING "WHO BUYS?" "WHO CARES?" & "WHAT MATTERS?"

1. Nicholas Toman, Brent Adamson, and Gomez, Cristina, "The New Sales Imperative," *Harvard Business Review*, March-April 2017, 3.
2. Brent Adamson, Matthew Dixon, Pat Spenner and Nick Toman, *The Challenger Customer: Selling to the Hidden Influencer Who Can Multiply Your Result,* (Portfolio Publishing, 2015).
3. Robert B. Miller, Stephen E. Heiman, and Tad Tuleja, *The New Strategic Selling: The Ultimate Sales System Proven Successful by the World's Best Companies*, (Grand Central Publishing, 2005), 82-102.
4. Mike Schultz, "5 Decision Roles in Every Sale," *Rain Group* (Blog), 2017, https://www.rainsalestraining.com/blog/5-decision-roles-in-every-sale, 2.
5. Hank Barnes, "The Journey to B2B Technology Purchases—B2B Team
6. "Buying Thickens the Plot," *Gartner Blog Network* (Blog), 2014, 2.
7. Mark Shonka and Dan Kosch, *Beyond Selling Value*, (Dearborn Trade Publishing, 2002), 57.
8. Bob Apollo, "Critical to B2B Sales Success—Stakeholder Assessments," *Selling in the Breakthrough Zone* (Blog), 2017 http://www.inflexion-point.com/blog/critical-to-b2b-sales-success-stakeholder-assessments.

9. Robert B. Miller, Stephen E. Heiman, *Strategic Selling,* (Warner Books, 1985). While *Strategic Selling* does not mention the "blue sheet" specifically, the book outlines all of the concepts involved in the creation of a strategic analysis plan (referred to as a blue sheet).

CHAPTER 2: BLOCKING & TACKLING: PLANNING & EXECUTING YOUR CUSTOMER-FOCUSED CONVERSATIONS

No Notes

CHAPTER 3: SELLING TO RESISTANT BUYERS: THE POWER OF INSIGHT-DRIVEN CONVERSATIONS

1. Mike Schultz, "What is Insight Selling?" *Rain Group* (Blog), 2017, https://www.rainsalestraining.com/blog/what-is-insight-selling, 1.
2. Richardson, "Selling with Insights Training." *Richardson* (Blog), 2018, https://www.richardson.com/sales-training-programs/insight-selling-training/ 1.
3. Mike Kunkle, "Why Selling Is a Joke," *Richardson* (Blog), January 27, 2014, 1.
4. Miller Heiman Group Research Report, "The 2016 Sales Enablement Optimization Study," *CSO Insights*, 2016.
5. Miller Heiman Group Research Report, "The 2017 Sales Enablement Optimization Study," *CSO Insights*, 2017.
6. Philip Lay, Todd Hewlin, and Geoffrey Moore, "In a Downturn, Provoke Your Customers," *Harvard Business Review*, 2009.
7. Corporate Visions, "To Challenge or Not to Challenge," *Corporate Visions* (ebook), 1.
8. Corporate Visions, "To Challenge," 7.
9. Corporate Visions, "To Challenge," 17.

CHAPTER 4: ROAD BLOCKS, POTHOLES & SPEED BUMPS: WHY SALES CALLS FAIL

1. Stephen Covey, *Good Reads*, https://www.goodreads.com/quotes/298301-most-people-do-not-listen-with-the-intent-to-understandDictionary.com.
2. Mark Twain, *AZ Quotes*, http://www.azquotes.com/quote/547855.
3. Peter Drucker, *Brainy Quote*, https://www.brainyquote.com/quotes/peter_drucker_142500.
4. Albert Einstein, *Brainy Quote*, https://www.brainyquote.com/quotes/albert_einstein_106192.

CHAPTER 5: FROM GATEKEEPER & BLOCKER TO MAP MAKER & GUIDE: GETTING PAST THE GATEKEEPER

1. Stephanie Scheller, *Getting Past the Gatekeeper: How to Turn Your Greatest Enemy Into Your Greatest Ally*, (Scheller Enterprises, 2016).

CHAPTER 6: BETTER EAT YOUR WHEATIES: SELLING AGAINST THE STATUS QUO

1. CSO Insights, "Sales Performance Optimization Study and Key Trends Analysis," *CSO Report* 2015.
2. Tamara Schenk, "Value Messaging and Why It's Key to Sales Enablement," Sales Enablement Perspectives (Blog), May 11, 2018, http://blog.tamaraschenk.com/value-messaging-and-why-it's-key-to-sales-enablement/.
3. Anthony Iannarino, "Your Client Is in Discovery, Too," *Iannarino* (Blog), January 8, 2014, http://thesalesblog.com/2014/01/08/your-client-is-in-discovery-too/.
4. Corporate Executive Board Study, *CEB* 2015 https://corporatevisions.com/why-now/.
5. Corporate Executive Board Study, *CEB* 2015 https://corporatevisions.com/why-now/.

6. Peter Noel Murray, "The Emotions of Luxury," *Psychology Today,* October 12, 2016, https://www.psychologytoday.com/blog/inside-the-consumer-mind/201610/the-emotions-luxury.

7. Philip Kotler. *AZQuotes,* http://www.azquotes.com/author/20187-Philip_Kotler.

8. Corporate Executive Board Study, *CEB* 2015 https://corporatevisions.com/why-now/.

CHAPTER 7: SURVIVING & WINNING BEAUTY CONTESTS (RFP PROCESSES)

No Notes

CHAPTER 8: INSIDE THE BLACK BOX: HARSH REALITIES OF SELLING TO A COMMITTEE

1. David Hoffeld, "3 Science-Backed Strategies to Improve Sales Effectiveness." Hubspot (Blog), October, 2016 https://blog.hubspot.com/sales/science-backed-strategies-to-improve-sales-effectiveness, 1.

2. Karl Schmidt, Brent Adamson, and Anna Bird, "Making the Consensus Sale," *Harvard Business Review*, 2015, https://hbr.org/2015/03/making-the-consensus-sale, 1.

3. Schmidt. "Making the Consensus Sale." 3.

4. Schmidt. "Making the Consensus Sale." 4.

5. Schmidt. "Making the Consensus Sale." 3.

6. Schmidt, "Making the Consensus Sale." 3.

7. Schmidt, "Making the Consensus Sale." 3.

CHAPTER 9: FRENEMIES: PARTNERING WITH PROCUREMENT

1. Chris Cliffe, "Why Buyer/Supplier Relationships Really Matter." e-Procurement News (Blog), March 26, 2017, http://www.novo-k.com/media/1292/chris-cliffe-inprocurement-magazine-buyer-supplier-relationships.pdf.

2. Peter Kraljic, "Purchasing Must Become Supply Management," *Harvard Business Review*, 1983, 109-117.

CHAPTER 10: THE PRICE IS NEVER RIGHT: MANAGING DISCOUNT DEMANDS

1. Brian Mandell, "Dealing with Obstacles and Complicating Factors," Program on Negotiation at Harvard Law School, *You Tube Video*. 2011.

Build Your
Professional Library

CHAPTER 1: SELLING TO MULTIPLE BUYERS: "WHO BUYS?" "WHO CARES?" "WHAT MATTERS?"

Bosworth, Michael T., and John R. Holland. *Customer Centric Selling.* McGraw-Hill, 2004.

Gielda, Steve, and Kevin Jones. *Premeditated Selling: Tools for Developing the Right Strategy.* ASTD Press, 2012.

Miller, Robert B., and Stephen E. Heiman. *The New Strategic Selling: The Unique Sales System Proven Successful by the World's Best Companies.* Grand Central Publishing, 2008.

Muir, James. *The Perfect Close: Secrets to Closing.* Best Practices International, 2016.

Page, Rick. *Hope is Not a Strategy: The Six Keys to Winning the Complex Sale.* McGraw Hill, 2003.

Shonka, Mark, and Dan Kosch. *Beyond Selling Value.* Dearborn Trade Publishing, 2002.

CHAPTER 2: PLANNING & EXECUTING YOUR CUSTOMER-FOCUSED CONVERSATIONS

Calvert, Deb. *Discover* Questions Get You Connected for Professional Sellers.* Winston Keen James Publishing, 2012, 2017.

Hoskins, John. *Level Five Selling: The Anatomy of a Quality Sales Call Revealed!* The First Advantage, LLC, 2016.

Iannarino, Anthony. Weekly blog. https://thesalesblog.com.

Keenan, Jim. *Not Taught: What It Takes to be Successful in the 21st Century that Nobody's Teaching You.* Self-Published, 2015.

Lindwall, Mark. "Why Don't Buyers Want to Meet With Your Salespeople?" *Forrester Blog.* September 29, 2014. https://go.forrester.com/blogs/14-09-29-why_dont_buyers_want_to_meet_with_your_salespeople.

Miller, Robert B., and Stephen E. Heiman. *The New Conceptual Selling: The Most Effective and Proven Method for Face-to-Face Sales Planning.* Kagan Page, 2012.

Nick, Michael J. *The Key to the C-Suite.* AMACOM Press, 2011.

Parinello, Antonio. *Selling to Vito: The Very Important Top Officer.* Adams Media Corporation, 1994.

Read, Nicholas A. C., and Stephen J. Bistritz. *Selling to the C-Suite.* McGraw Hill, 2018.

CHAPTER 3: SELLING TO RESISTANT BUYERS: THE POWER OF INSIGHT-DRIVEN CONVERSATIONS

Blount, Jeb. *Sales EQ: How Ultra High Performers Leverage Sales-Specific Emotional Intelligence to Close the Complex Sale.* Wiley, 2017.

Cohen, Elay. *Sales Hood: How Winning Sales Managers Inspire Sales Teams to Succeed.* Greenleaf Book Group Press, 2014.

Harris, Michael. *Insight Selling: How to Sell Value and Differentiate Your Product with Insight Scenarios.* Sales and Marketing Press, 2014.

Konrath, Jill. *Snap Selling: Speed Up Sales and Win More Business with Today's Frazzled Customers.* Penguin Group, 2010.

Miller, Robert. *The New Conceptual Selling: The Most Effective and Proven Method of Face-to-Face Sales Planning.* Kagan Page, 2012.

Schultz, Mike, and John E. Doerr. *Insight Selling: Surprising Research on What Sales Winners Do Differently.* Wiley, 2014.

Schultz, Mike, and John E. Doerr. *Rainmaker Conversations: Influence, Persuade and Sell in Any Situation.* AMACOM, 2011.

Weinberg, Mike, and Anthony S. Iannarino. *New Sales. Simplified: The Essential Handbook for Prospecting and New Sales Development.* AMACOM, 2012.

CHAPTER 4: ROAD BLOCKS, POTHOLES & SPEED BUMPS: WHY SALES CALLS FAIL

Blount, Jeb. *Fanatical Prospecting: The Ultimate Guide to Opening and Filling Pipeline by Leveraging Social Selling.* Wiley and Sons, 2015.

Dixon, Matthew, and Brent Adamson. *The Challenger Sale: Taking Control of the Customer Conversation.* Penguin Group, 2011.

Richardson, Linda. *Changing the Sales Conversation: Connect, Collaborate and Close.* McGraw-Hill Education, 2013.

CHAPTER 5: FROM GATEKEEPER & BLOCKER TO MAPMAKER & GUIDE

Dickens, Andy. "Top Ten Tips for Getting Past the Gatekeeper." VSL Sales Driven, February, 2015. https://www.virtual-sales.com/top-ten-tips-for-getting-past-the-gatekeeper.

Johnson, Bill. "7 Must-Dos to Get Past the Gatekeeper." LeadJen, November, 2013. https://www.leadjen.com/7-must-dos-to-get-past-the-gatekeeper.

CHAPTER 6: BETTER EAT YOUR WHEATIES: SELLING AGAINST THE STATUS QUO

Andersen Steve and Dave Stein. *Beyond the Sales Process: 12 Proven Strategies for a Customer-Driven World.* AMACOM, 2016.

Brudnes, Emma. "How to Use Emotions to Sell." *Hubspot Blog.* April, 2015. https://blog.hubspot.com/sales/how-to-use-emotions-to-sell.

Hansen, Julie. "3 Powerful Ways to Sell Against the Status Quo in Your Presentation." *Storytelling Blog.* July, 2016. http://performancesalesandtraining.com/3-ways-sell-against-the-status-quo.

Harris, Michael D. "When to Sell with Facts and Figures, and When to Appeal to Emotions," *Harvard Business Review,* 2015. https://hbr.org/2015/01/when-to-sell-with-facts-and-figures-and-when-to-appeal-to-emotions.

Iannarino, Anthony. *The Lost Art of Closing: Winning the Ten Commitments that Drive Sales.* Portfolio. 2017.

Murray, Peter Noel. "The Emotions of Luxury," *Psychology Today*, October, 2016. https://www.psychologytoday.com/blog/inside-the-consumer-mind/201610/the-emotions-luxury.

Morin, Amy. "Your Competition Isn't Your Real Competitor: Status Quo Is," *Forbes Blog.* March, 2014.

Nardin, Nancy. "Sellers and Marketers Overcoming the Status Quo," Smart Selling Tools, July, 2016. https://smartsellingtools.com/overcoming-the-status-quo.

Nathan, Sam, and Karl Schmidt. "From Promotions to Emotion: Connecting B2B Customers to Brands." *Google Blog.* October, 2013. https://www.cebglobal.com/marketing-communications/b2b-emotion.html.

PersistIQ. "How to Sell More Using 5 Primal Human Emotions," The *PersistIQ* Sales Blog, December, 2015. http://blog.persistiq.com/how-to-sell-more-using-5-primal-human-emotions.

Petersen, Erik, and Tim Riesterer. *Conversations That Win The Complex Sale: Using Power Messaging to Create More Opportunities, Differentiate Your Solutions and Close More Deals.* McGraw-Hill, 2011.

Pinci, Larry, and Phil Grosserman. *Sell the Feeling: The Six-Step System That Drives People to Do Business with You.* Morgan James Press, 2008.

Schultz, Mike and John E. Doerr. *Insight Selling: Surprising Research on What Sales Winners Do Differently.* Wiley, 2014.

CHAPTER 7: COMPETING & WINNING BEAUTY CONTESTS (RFP PROCESSES)

Deeb, George. "The 10 Things You Need to Know When Responding to RFPs." *Entrepreneur Blog.* October, 2013. https://www.entrepreneur.com/article/252061.

Kay, Marianne. "How to Respond to an RFP." *J. Boye Blog.* 2013. https://www.slideshare.net/MarianneKolodiy/how-torespondtorfp.

Quote-Roller. "Red-Hot Tips on How to Respond to an RFP and Win That Deal." (blog). 2013. https://blog.quoteroller.com/how-to-respond-to-request-for-proposal/.

Searcy, Tom. *RFPs Suck! How to Master the RFP System Once and For All to Win Big Business.* Channel V Books, 2009.

Spear, Todd. "12 Tips to Help You Respond to an RFP With No Fear." PandaDoc. 2014. https://lexcis.com/blogs/12-tips-to-help-you-respond-to-a-rfp-with-no-fear/

Warrillow, John. "Death by RFP: 7 Reasons Not to Respond." *Inc. Blog.* March, 2013. https://www.inc.com/john-warrillow/death-by-rfp-seven-reasons-not-to-respond.html.

CHAPTER 8: INSIDE THE BLACK BOX: HARSH REALITIES OF SELLING TO A COMMITTEE

Dalis, Mike. S. *Sell Like a Team: The Blueprint for Building Teams that Win Big at High-Stakes Meetings.* McGraw-Hill. 2017.

Enns, Blair. "Selling to Committees." *Win Without Pitching Blog.* https://www.winwithoutpitching.com/selling-to-committees.

Givens, Leonard L. "A Survival Guide to Selling to Committees—Part 1." *Quest Blog.* https://www.questteam.com/resources/article.html?id=given_article_3.

Miller, Robert B., and Gary A. Williams. *The 5 Paths to Persuasion: The Art of Selling Your Message.* Grand Central Publishing, 2007.

Nanigian, Greg. "Selling to Groups and Committees," *Ezine Articles,* 2011.

CHAPTER 9: FRENEMIES: PARTNERING WITH PROCUREMENT

APICS. "Transforming Procurement into a Global Powerhouse." *APICS Blog.* 2017. http://www.supplychain247.com/paper/transforming_procurement_into_a_global_powerhouse_the_mccormick_journey.

Dominick, Charles. "Suppliers' Secrets for Negotiating With Purchasing." NLPA. https://www.nextlevelpurchasing.com/articles/negotiating-purchasing.php.

Makela, Ray. "5 Sales Counter-Tactics When Negotiating with Purchasing." *SalesForce Blog*. 2015. https://www.salesforce.com/blog/2015/01/5-sales-counter-tactics-when-negotiating-procurement-gp.html.

Murray, Martin. "Negotiation in the Purchasing Process." *The Balance Blog*. 2017. https://www.thebalance.com/negotiation-in-the-purchasing-process-2221379.

Trowbridge, Mark. "Seven Techniques for Preparing Winning Negotiations With Your Key Suppliers." *Supply Chain Blog*. 2013. https://www.linkedin.com/pulse/seven-techniques-preparing-winning-negotiations-your-key-rahman.

CHAPTER 10: THE PRICE IS NEVER RIGHT: MANAGING DISCOUNT DEMANDS

Camp, Jim. *Start With No: The Negotiation Tools That Pros Don't Want You to Know*. Crown Business, 2011.

Fisher, Roger, William L. Ury, and Bruce Patton. *Getting to Yes: Negotiating Agreement Without Giving In*. Penguin Books, 2011.

Leuck, Richard. *Negotiation (Harvard Business Essentials)*. Harvard Business School Press, 2003.

Lum, Grande. *The Negotiation Fieldbook: Simple Strategies to Help You Negotiate Everything*. McGraw-Hill, 2005.

Tinney, Patrick. *Unlocking Yes: Sales Negotiation Lessons and Strategy*. Centroid Publishing. 2015.

Voss, Chris, and Tahl Razl. *Never Split the Difference: Negotiating as If Your Life Depended on It*. Harper Business, 2016.

Acknowledgements

This book would have never been completed without the life and work experiences afforded to both of us. Each job, company, employee, channel member, and customer played a role in our learning, thinking, and writing.

We would especially like to thank Nancy Williams and Vicki Hodges for their support and companionship.

We would also like to thank all our reviewers who took the time and energy to provide their feedback and suggestions to improve the quality of our content. Your insight was invaluable, and we can never thank you enough for your contributions.

A special thank you to: James Welsh, Brenda Irwin, Dave Canham, Len Serafino, Mickey Neverman, Jon Szobody, Tamara Schenk, Rich Blakeman, Joe Galvin, Scott Marans, Paul Fornelli, Mike Joyce Sr., Dana Palmblad, Bill Golder, Michael Spence, Andrew Lambert, Rick Drake, Chris Woolway, James Robberstad, Al Kepler, Bob Hatcher, Bob Peisert, Pascale Hall, Erin Elsasser, Heather L. Williams, Thomas M. Williams, and George Ellis.

In every book, there is someone behind the scenes who applies the deft touches that brings the manuscript alive—making the manuscript clear, readable, and engaging. Our "wizard" is Mary Jo Gensemer. Thanks, M.J.

We would also like to thank Glenn Marshall of Greening Marketing and his team for the cover design and 1106 Design for turning our manuscript into reality. We are indebted to all of you.

Last, we would like to thank you, the reader, for reading our book. We will consider this missive a success if we help you close one more profitable deal or increase your win rate.

Good Selling!

Tom Williams

Tom Saine

About Us

 Tom Williams is the Managing Director of Strategic Dynamics Inc., a firm that helps organizations accelerate revenue generation. He was formerly Vice President of Worldwide Sales, Marketing and Product Service for an organization that sold high-technology medical products and services through a variety of distribution channels, the CEO of two specialty hospitals, the Vice President and General Manager of an ancillary services division, and the President of a medical services company. Tom has a B.S. in Biology from the University of Detroit, and a MAM (Master's degree in Management) and MBA from the Peter F. Drucker and Masatoshi Ito Graduate School of Management at Claremont Graduate University. He is also a registered and certified Respiratory Therapist. Additionally, Tom is a certified facilitator in most of the Miller Heiman Group methodologies. He routinely sells their services, conducts program facilitation, and provides consulting around their various sales methodologies. Tom is recognized for his expertise in call planning and execution, opportunity management, negotiation, key account management, funnel management, sales coaching and selling to the C-suite. Tom is also the co-author of *Selling to Hospitals and Healthcare Organizations: A Glossary of Business Acumen and Personnel.*

 Tom Saine is a Senior Consultant with Strategic Dynamics Inc. with a Ph.D. in Communication from Northwestern University. He is a former senior executive for ARAMARK Corporation. In his tenure with ARAMARK, Tom served as Associate Vice President for Major Account Sales, Vice President of Client Retention, and Vice President of Sales. His background in sales management for ARAMARK includes supervising direct sales for the U.S. and Canada, developing the division's strategic plan, and creating a master plan for retaining business.

Prior to his years at ARAMARK, Tom was on the faculty of the University of Florida and the University of Denver. Tom has published extensively on group communication, decision-making, negotiation, and organizational communication. In 2007, he joined the team at the Miller Heiman Group as a Senior Consultant helping customers optimize sales growth and productivity. Tom assists executives in forging strategic sales plans and enhancing the skill sets of their frontline sales team. Tom has extensive sales enablement experience in such areas as key account management and retention, sales strategy, prospecting skills, closing deals, and negotiating complex contracts.

Contact Information

Phone: 951-515-8159
Website: StrategicDynamicsFirm.com
E-Mail: TWilliams@StrategicDynamicsFirm.com
E-Mail: TSaine@StrategicDynamicsFirm.com

Connect with Us!

LinkedIn—Tom Williams: www.linkedin.com/in/thomasjwilliams
LinkedIn—Tom Saine: www.linkedin.com/pub/tom-saine/94/3a/7b6
Twitter: SD_Firm
Blog: http://strategicdynamicsfirm.com/blog/
Facebook: https://www.facebook.com/StrategicDynamicsFirm

Training, Workshops and Speaking Engagements

Strategic Dynamics Inc. is a sales productivity improvement company. The firm provides a range of services that includes: strategy, market research and analysis, sales process engineering, sales force evaluation, tools to hire and retain employees and sales training.

Our sales training programs and workshops are for sales professionals, leaders, and account executives. Our training media, educational design, and delivery format is engaging and designed to meet multi-generational learning styles and preferences. We blend adult learning principles with interactive facilitation and experiential learning, mini-workshops, and role-plays to anchor key concepts and drive comprehension and adoption.

We are also available for speaking engagements at local, regional, and national events. To discuss your needs, please reach out to us directly or via info@StrategicDynamicsFirm.com.

Free Additional Resources

Readers will also find available a complementary Companion Workbook that will help them reinforce and cement the key concepts of the book into their sales DNA. All the figures, tables, checklists, and other resources shown or listed in the book are available on our website at www.StrategicDynamicsFirm.com. Please feel free to download and use any of the material that you find useful. When you do so, please give attribution to *The Sellers Challenge: How Top Sellers Master 10 Deal Killing Obstacles in B2B Sales.*

We will continue to add additional resources, so please visit our website and check back often.

Index

Write a Book Review

Both of us hope that you found the book interesting, informative, and insightful. Our goal was to help you overcome the most common challenges by providing an in-depth perspective to both the problem and the solution based on our years of successful and unsuccessful experiences.

Please share your thoughts on our book with your colleagues by writing a thoughtful review. Readers appreciate hearing from their peers about whether a book is worthwhile to read or not.

As you write your review, please consider the following:

- Was the writing clear, concise, and understandable?
- Was the content presented in an engaging and conversational manner?
- Could you identify with the challenges?
- Did the sales stories provide good examples of real-life selling situations?
- Was the content presented in the Addendums helpful?
- What was the one most beneficial takeaway that you had from this book?
- Who could best benefit from reading this book?
- What makes this book different from others in its genre?

What will you do differently now that you have read this book?